The Cheesecake Cookbook Bible

1000 Days of Light and Creamy Cheesecake Recipes

that Will Make You Grin for Hours

Chrissie Rolove

© **Copyright 2022 - All rights reserved.**

The content contained within this book may not be reproduced, duplicated, or transmitted without direct written permission from the author or the publisher.

Under no circumstances will any blame or legal responsibility be held against the publisher, or author, for any damages, reparation, or monetary loss due to the information contained within this book. Either directly or indirectly.

Legal Notice:

This book is copyright protected. This book is only for personal use. You cannot amend, distribute, sell, use, quote, or paraphrase any part, or the content within this book, without the consent of the author or publisher.

Disclaimer Notice:

By reading this document, the reader agrees that under no circumstances is the author responsible for any losses, direct or indirect, which are incurred as a result of the use of the information contained within this document, including, but not limited to, - errors, omissions, or inaccuracies.

The information contained in this book and its contents is not designed to replace or take the place of any form of medical or professional advice; and is not meant to replace the need for independent medical, financial, legal or other professional advice or services, as may be required. The content and information in this book have been provided for educational and entertainment purposes only.

Table of Contents

introduction 6

Chapter 1: Tips And Tricks 8

Chapter 2: Ingredients For A Perfect Cheesecake 11

Chapter 3: Equipment And Tools 14

Chapter 4: 110 Recipes 16

    1. MANGO AND COCONUT CHEESECAKE 17
    2. MIXED BERRY CHEESECAKE 18
    3. PASSIONFRUIT CHEESECAKE 20
    4. PINEAPPLE CHEESECAKE 21
    5. RASPBERRY CHEESECAKE 22
    6. STRAWBERRY CHEESECAKE (WITH A FEW RASPBERRIES) 23
    7. NEW YORK BAKED CHEESECAKE 24
    8. OREO CHEESECAKE 25
    9. RED VELVET CHEESECAKE 26
    10. CLASSIC CHEESECAKE 28
    11. COCONUT CARDAMOM CHEESECAKE 29
    12. CONCORDE GRAPE CHEESECAKE WITH FIG AND GRAPE PUREE 30
    13. CRANBERRY GRAPE CHEESECAKE 31
    14. DOUBLE CHOCOLATE CHERRY CHEESECAKE 32
    15. DOUBLE CRUSTED PUMPKIN CHOCOLATE CHEESECAKE 33
    16. KEY LIME CHEESECAKE WITH COCONUT CREAM TOPPING 34
    17. LEMON BERRY SWIRL CHEESECAKE 35
    18. SWEET KALE CHEESECAKE 36
    19. TIRAMISU WITH VANILLA CREAM AND COFFEE LADYFINGERS 37
    20. TRIPLE BERRY SWIRL CHEESECAKE 38
    21. VANILLA CHOCOLATE BROWNIE CHEESECAKE WITH STRAWBERRY SAUCE 39
    22. VANILLA LEMON CHEESECAKE 41
    23. CHOCOLATE QUARK CHEESECAKE 42
    24. CHOCOLATE CHEESECAKE 44
    25. CARROT CAKE CHEESECAKE 45
    26. FRUIT CHEESECAKE PIE 47
    27. NUTELLA OREO CHEESECAKE 48
    28. CARAMEL CHEESECAKE 49
    29. BERRY-RICOTTA CHEESECAKE 50
    30. BANANA CREAM CHEESECAKE 52
    31. PISTACHIO CHEESECAKE 53
    32. CARROT CHEESECAKE 54
    33. CHOCOLATE CUPCAKES WITH PUMPKIN CHEESECAKE FILLING 55
    34. CHOCOLATE PEANUT BUTTER CHEESECAKE CUPS 56
    35. DOUBLE CARAMEL PECAN CHEESECAKE BARS 57
    36. EASY SOUR CREAM CHEESECAKE 58
    37. EASY STRAWBERRY CHEESECAKE 59
    38. FIG HAZELNUT CHEESECAKE WITH HONEY BOURBON DRIZZLE 60
    39. FIVE STAR CHEESECAKE 62
    40. FROSTED CREAM CHEESE BROWNIES 63
    41. BERRY-TOPPED CHEESECAKE 64
    42. BEST EVER CHEESECAKE 65

43. Birthday Cake Cheesecake 66
44. Black Forest Cheesecake 67
45. Blackberry Cheesecake Cups 68
46. Brown Sugar Amaretto Cheesecake 69
47. Brownie Chocolate Chip Cheesecake 70
48. Butter Pecan Cheesecake 71
49. Butterfinger Cheesecake 72
50. Candy Bar Cheesecake 73
51. Candy Cane Cheesecake 75
52. Red Velvet Cheesecake 76
53. Pina Colada Cheesecake 77
54. Triple Chocolate Cheesecake 79
55. Cinnamon Roll Cheesecake 80
56. Classic Strawberry Cheesecake 82
57. Pumpkin Cheesecake Bars 83
58. Reese's Cheesecake 84
59. Caramel Cheesecake Bars 85
60. Eggnog Cheesecake 86
61. Lemon Bar Cheesecake 87
62. Lemon Cheesecake 88
63. Vanilla Cheesecake 89
64. Chocolate Cheesecake 90
65. Delicious Chocó Cheesecake 91
66. Almond Cheesecake 92
67. Ricotta Lemon Cheesecake 93
68. Vanilla Cheesecake 94
69. Lemon Cheesecake In Mugs 95
70. Blueberry Cheesecake 96
71. Pumpkin Cheesecake 97
72. Matcha Cheesecake 98
73. Classic Pound Cake 99
74. Moist Carrot Cake 100
75. Gooey & Rich Butter Cake 101
76. Lemon Pound Cake 102
77. Simple Chocolate Cake 103
78. Perfect Pumpkin Crumb Cake 104
79. Carrot Cake With Frosting 105
80. Chocolate Flourless Cake 106
81. Light & Fluffy Coffee Cake 107
82. Moist Coconut Pound Cake 108
83. Super Easy Chocolate Cake 109
84. Cream Cheese Pound Cake 110
85. Moist Vanilla Cake 111
86. Perfect Blackberry Cake 112
87. Perfect Gingerbread Cake 113
88. Chocolate Zucchini Cake 114
89. Perfect Almond Crumb Cake 115
90. Lemon Pound Cake 116
91. Blueberry Cake 117
92. Brownie Mug Cake 118
93. Peanut Butter Mug Cake 119
94. Vanilla Mug Cake 120
95. Delicious Berry Cake 121

96. QUICK MICROWAVE CHEESECAKE ... 122
97. EASY LEMON CHEESECAKE ... 123
98. DELICIOUS & HEALTHY PUMPKIN CHEESECAKE ... 124
99. ALMOND COCONUT CHEESECAKE ... 125
100. ALMOND CAKE ... 126
101. MOIST VANILLA CAKE ... 127
102. BASIC CHEESE CAKE ... 128
103. QUICK & EASY CHEESECAKE ... 129
104. ITALIAN CHEESECAKE ... 130
105. ITALIAN CREAMY CAKE ... 131
106. SICILIAN LAYER CAKE ... 132
107. RICOTTA CINNAMON CHEESECAKE ... 133
108. BLUEBERRY CHEESE SQUARES ... 134
109. CHOCOLATE ITALIAN CREAM CAKE ... 135
110. ITALIAN ANNIVERSARY CAKE ... 136

Chapter 5: Faqs ... **137**
WHAT INGREDIENT SUBSTITUTIONS CAN YOU MAKE? ... 137
HOW TO DO A PERFECT CRUST PRESENTATION? ... 138
HOW TO DO PROPER PROCESSING / MIXING? ... 138
HOW TO MASTER TIMES AND TEMPERATURES? ... 139
HOW TO KNOW SIGNS OF DONENESS? ... 139
HOW CAN YOU PREVENT CRACKING? ... 139
HOW TO MASTER TOPPING PRESENTATION? ... 140
HOW TO PREPARE THE CHEESECAKE FOR SERVING? ... 141
HOW TO APPLY THE RECIPE CONVERSION FACTORS? ... 142

Conclusion ... **143**

Alphabetical Index ... **144**

INTRODUCTION

Cheesecake is a versatile dessert that comes in a variety of flavors. If you're craving cheesecake for breakfast, a nice glass of cheesecake parfait is the best thing to make. One intriguing aspect of cheesecake is that it is a baked cheese custard with a crust rather than a cake. Nobody can resist its delicate flavor and texture, whatever you call it. It's so well-liked here that June 4th is designated as National Cheesecake Day.

The book's main goal is to provide you with simple cheesecake recipes that you could easily make at home for your loved ones. All recipes have been tried and tested, and we can attest to their ability to transport your taste buds to dessert heaven.

However, the recipes in this book are just our ideas, and you can play around with them as much as you want to create your own unique recipes. In fact, you can enlist the assistance of your children. Not only will they have a good time in the kitchen, but it will also help bring out their creativity.

Even though it appears to be a simple dessert to make, and it is, there are a few things to keep in mind when preparing this delectable, decadent, and delicate dessert.

First and foremost, the baked cheesecake is the original, and it's every bit as crunchy and sweet as it sounds. To keep the filling in the graham cracker shell, a graham cracker crust sweetened with granulated sugar and mixed with melted butter is always pressed into the bottom and sides of an 8-9 inch springform pan. The crust must be baked, but be careful not to overbake it. You don't want it to taste bitter, which could happen otherwise.

Second, make sure to thoroughly combine the cream cheese filling ingredients to create a smooth and creamy filling free of lumps. By doing this, you can make the most of this exquisite dessert.

One of the most important things to remember is that the cheesecake should not be overbaked or underbaked. Underbaking it is more dangerous because if you cut a slice of underbaked cheesecake, it will spill all over the table, which is not what you want. If you overbake the cheesecake, the best way to cover it is with whipped cream, but if the chocolate goes well with the other ingredients, a chocolate glaze will suffice. Whipped cream is always a good idea because, let's face it, who doesn't enjoy whipped cream with anything sweet?

Add cornstarch or flour to the cream cheese filling to ensure that the cheesecake sets while baking. A little goes a long way in this case, so don't use more than 14-12 cup flour in your filling. Finally, if your cheesecake becomes too brown on top and still jiggles when you shake the springform pan, cover the top with aluminum foil or reduce the temperature and bake for a longer period of time.

Giving your cheesecake a final touch will make it look more appealing than when served plain. To add a nice finishing touch, use whipped cream, caramel sauce, chocolate glaze, fresh fruit, or simply sprinkle something on top. To be honest, some cheesecakes taste better without any fancy extra ingredients on top.

A perfect cheese cake does not necessitate the use of exotic ingredients. To decorate your masterpiece, use simple ingredients such as fresh fruit, nuts, or food coloring. But when constructing a cheesecake, cream cheese and sour cream are two of the most crucial ingredients. Similar to that, you need a crumbled biscuit crust with butter and sugar.

You can also use some gelatin to get a jelly-like texture for the cake. Additionally, you can experiment using various food colors and extracts to add that extra oomph to your cheesecakes.

CHAPTER 1: TIPS AND TRICKS

Always gather all of your ingredients before beginning the recipe; this way, you won't be scratching around for some of the ingredients. You should grease the bottom and sides of your baking pan or tin and place nonstick baking paper on the bottom.

Don't worry if your cheesecake isn't perfect; a layer of fruit sprinkled on top will cover up any cracks.

Always crush your biscuits to fine crumbs; otherwise, the base may not set properly, making it difficult to cut.

Cheesecakes bake better in a conventional oven, so if your oven is fan forced and you can't turn the fan off, reduce the temperature by 20°C for all baked recipes. I attempted to include temperatures for all different types of ovens in each recipe; please accept my apologies if I missed any.

If your recipe calls for baking the cheesecake rather than chilling it, don't overbeat the mixture and bake it in the lower half of the oven. Cool your baked cheesecake in the oven for an hour after cooking and before removing it from the oven by turning off the oven and leaving the door slightly open.

Chill your baked cheesecake in the fridge after it has completely cooled for a really firm result.

If a recipe calls for shaved coconut and you can't find it, try a health food store or an Asian grocer. Otherwise, crack open a fresh coconut, carefully pry out the flesh with a sharp object, shave with a vegetable peeler, and toast in a slow oven for about 25 minutes, or until golden in color. Keep it in an airtight container and it will be ready when you need it. It will last a few weeks if done in this manner. Because coconut might spoil, it shouldn't be kept for an extended period of time.

Do you understand the distinctions between zest, rind, and peel? Zests are long, thin curls of rind packed with flavor; a zesting tool is ideal for this. Grating rind requires the use of a fine grating tool. Often used in baking and sauces, rind can also be tossed through pasta to add a bit of zing. Use a vegetable peeler to get long thin curls of rind for decoration, being careful not to get any of the pith as this will add a bitter taste to your dish.

Chilled cheesecakes are great for cooking with kids; just be careful when dissolving the gelatin in the hot water; you really need to do this for them, or use flavored jelly instead.

Pour the gelatin into your mixture through a small tea or coffee strainer that has been heated in hot water to ensure that the gelatin is added lump free.

You can add any fruit of your choice to any of the bases (sliced bananas dipped in lemon juice are very tasty - you need the lemon juice to keep the bananas from turning brown), a layer of strawberries is beautiful, but I would recommend that you cover the base first with a thin layer of melted chocolate to form a barrier and keep the biscuit base from becoming soggy. This can be done before pouring over your preferred recipe. You can also do this with baked cheesecake (except for the melted chocolate), but don't put too much on because it can seep through.

If you're making a frozen cheesecake, make a space in the freezer ahead of time so you don't have to struggle to put it in the freezer once it's done.

When making a lemon or lime chilled cheesecake, try slicing the fruit very thinly and placing it around the side of the tin before pouring in the filling so that the sides are nicely decorated with slices of the fruit when you take it out of the tin.

Avoid overbeating the cream cheese because doing so will add too much air to the mixture and make your cheesecake crumble.

If you're using a gas oven, place your cheesecake on the lowest shelf, where it will be slightly cooler. Place your electric oven in the middle of the room to avoid any touch with the heating elements.

Your cheesecake is finished when the sides are puffy but the middle is still somewhat unstable.

I always put a bowl of hot tap water at the bottom of my oven to keep it from burning and to keep the cheesecake from drying out.

Gelatin-based dishes typically require 6-8 hours in the refrigerator before serving.

This cookbook's recipes all call for 60g eggs. The butter is unsalted, but I've made many, many cheesecakes with regular butter and they haven't turned out bad.

Practically all of the recipes in this book can be prepared in advance and frozen. Once the cheesecake is cooled, remove the cheesecake from the baking pan/tin and freeze uncovered until the top is starting to freeze. (This saves the top from getting ice burns). It will last for about two months if you remove it from the freezer and wrap it in two layers of plastic wrap and one layer of foil. Do not decorate before you freeze the cheesecake. When you want to use the cheesecake, remove from the freeze and either thaw for several hours at room temperature or place in the fridge overnight and then you can decorate the cheesecake.

CHAPTER 2:
INGREDIENTS FOR A PERFECT CHEESECAKE

Butter

When used in baking recipes, butter greatly enhances the flavor and texture of the finished product. On its own, butter has an amazing flavor and texture. Because it provides you complete control over the flavor of your recipes, unsalted butter is great.

Milk

One of the most vital elements when it comes to baking is milk. It tenderizes the four and serves as the foundation for many recipes.

Flour

Before using flour in a baking recipe, always sift it. Almost any kind of flour can be used for baking, however "All Purpose Flour" is the most popular variety. It is widely accessible, reasonably priced, and easy to use.

"Cake Flour" is a smoother type of flour than all-purpose flour. It's excellent for creating cake sponges and other delicate baked products with a spongy texture.

"Pastry Flour" is another flour that functions similarly to cake flour.

Self-Rising Flour is all-purpose flour combined with baking powder. One teaspoon of baking powder per cup of flour should be used to produce your own.

"Rye Flour" is a high-protein flour with numerous nutritional benefits. However, because it does not produce gluten strands, it cannot be used in yeasted dough.

"Oat Flour" contains a lot of fiber and protein. It is frequently used in low-fat baking recipes.

Almond flour, coconut flour, and tapioca flour are some more types of flour used in baking today.

Baking Powder

Baking powder is made composed of baking soda and an acidic ingredient. It does not require an acidic ingredient to function as a leavening agent on its own.

Baking powder is produced by hundreds of different branks, all of which have the same appearance. Make sure the baking powder you buy is devoid of aluminum before you buy it. Before the baking powder's six-month shelf life expires, use it all up.

Baking Soda

A second acidic element must be added in order for baking soda to function as a leavening agent. It can be stored safely for a very long period.

Yeast

Bread, dinner rolls, and other pastries frequently contain yeast, a natural leavening agent. It ferments in the batter or dough to fulfill its purpose, absorbing air to expand the volume.

Sugar

Excess sugar causes an increase in blood glycogen levels and is to blame for a variety of health issues. Consume sugary treats sparingly and as an addition to a nutritious, well-balanced diet. Some baked goods require sugar as it gives them structure, sweetness, and moisture. It also promotes yeast growth in a few of the recipes.

There are numerous types of sugar available, and each recipe will specify the type of sugar used. If it is not specified, use regular granulated sugar. Brown sugar is unrefined white sugar with a distinct flavor that makes it unsuitable for most recipes. In some recipes, however, the flavor of brown sugar complements the flavor of the recipe.

Chocolate

Choose dark chocolate with at least a 70% cocoa content if a recipe in this book calls for it. Due to its low sugar content, robust flavor, and excellent texture, dark chocolate is the type that is used most frequently in this book. If a recipe calls for chocolate chips and you don't have any on hand, simply break up a bar of dark chocolate into tiny pieces.

White and milk chocolates are also popular these days, and they taste fantastic due to their high sugar content.

Cocoa Powder

The two most widely used types of cocoa powder on the market right now are natural and Dutch-processed variants.

Unless otherwise stated, all of the cocoa powder used in this book is Dutch-processed, giving it a richer, darker hue.

Eggs

The best eggs come from a free-range ranch. Except as otherwise specified, all eggs in this book are medium-sized.

Because they improve the texture of cakes and biscuits and allow air to enter the batter, eggs are a common ingredient in baking. This makes the batter fluffy. Additionally, they keep the dishes wet.

Eggs not only taste great and are nourishing on their own, but they also add flavor, color, and nutrients to baked items.

Gelatin

Gelatin, commonly known as collagen, is a clear, flavorless food component manufactured from the collagen of animal body parts. When it is dry, it is brittle, and when it is wet, it is sticky. It is used to stabilize creams and jellies and must bloom before use. It becomes weakened when boiled, therefore avoid doing so.

Unless otherwise stated, all of the gelatin in this book is powdered or granulated. Additionally, leafed gelatin can be helpful on occasion.

Nuts

Nuts are a great source of good fats and go great on virtually everything baked. In baked recipes, nuts like almonds, coconut, hazelnuts, pecans, peanuts, walnuts, pistachios, macadamia nuts, cashew nuts, and others are frequently utilized. The best nuts are the freshest.

Salt

All forms of cooking, including baking, frequently include salt. Salt is incredibly helpful with yeast since it helps the structure of the gluten and enhances flavor.

Spices

Spices give a range of tastes to baked goods and are both tasty and nourishing. Vanilla is one of the most widely used spices in baking. The greatest vanilla extract is natural. Other spices that are frequently used in baking include cinnamon, ginger, nutmeg, cardamom, orange zest, lemon zest, cloves, lavender, etc..

CHAPTER 3: EQUIPMENT AND TOOLS

Baking Pans

Small or large pans, they all do the job. Just be certain to keep some on hand.

Cake pans are very useful for baking cakes. You only actually need one pan if you don't want to bake several cakes at once. Typically, a basic pan with an eight to nine-inch diameter will do. They are widely available in retail outlets and on Amazon.

Bundt cake pans are used to create stunning shapes for your cakes. They come in a variety of shapes, sizes, and patterns. Just keep in mind that the more complex the design, the more difficult it is to clean.

Muffin tins are extremely useful for baking muffins and are widely available on Amazon and in local stores. Because I have a family of four, I prefer muffin tins with a minimum capacity of 12 cups. Simply reduce the amount of ingredients you use proportionally if you get a smaller one.

Pie and tart pans are also helpful little pans, and if you want to make these recipes, you should have at least one of each.

Mixer

Even while you can mix everything by hand using a spoon or whisk, having a mixer undoubtedly makes things simpler. Any compact mixer will do. It's actually not necessary, though, if you don't mind some manual whisking and stirring.

Whisk

When it comes to baking, whisks are a must-have tool. There are both manual and electronic whisks available today, and both will do the job.

Wooden Spoons and Spatulas

In order to avoid gluten threads from developing, some mixes must be blended gently, which is why spatulas and wooden spoons are usually useful.

Food Preparation Machine

Food processors are inexpensive and can make certain grinding tasks a breeze!

Spoons and Cups for Measuring

All recipes call for specific quantities of ingredients, so you'll need some measuring tools. If you've been cooking for a while, you're probably getting pretty good at estimating by now, but for new cooks, measuring tools are crucial.

If you don't already have one, purchase an American measuring set. One set includes all of the standard measurements mentioned in this book, and they are reasonably priced.

Bowls for Mixing

My favorite mixing containers are made of steel or glass.

Parchment or baking paper

Baking paper is essential for baking. In addition to preventing the ingredients from burning or baking too quickly, it also makes cleanup simple.

Springform Pans

Springform pans are typically available in sizes ranging from 7 to 12 inches; if you can only afford one, the 9-inch size is the most useful.

Double Boiler

A double boiler is useful for melting chocolate and other items.

Some other baking essentials: -

- Baking wax paper sheets
- Nonstick parchment paper
- Cooking spray
- Blender or food processor - for chopping crust ingredients
- Wire rack - for cooling hot from the oven cakes
- Grater - used to grate chocolate for garnishes.
- Microwave - useful for warming ingredients on occasion.
- Oven thermometer

Most of these tools are available in a well-stocked grocery store, department store, or a kitchen specialty store, or as a last resort, from a restaurant supply house.

CHAPTER 4: 110 RECIPES

1. Mango and Coconut Cheesecake

<u>Prep</u> **Time**: 10 minutes
Cooking Time: 60 minutes
Servings: 5
Ingredients:
- 125g (1cup) plain flour
- 100g (1.1/3 cup) desiccated coconut
- 100g (1/2 cup) butter
- 2 Tbsp. (30ml) lime juice
- 500g cream cheese at room temperature
- 200g coconut cream
- 200g (3/4 cup) caster/superfine sugar
- 3 eggs + 2 egg yolks
- 2 mangoes peeled, sliced to serve (or you could use a tin of sliced mangoes)
- 40g (1/2 cup) shaved coconut, toasted

Directions:
1. Preheat your oven to 180°C for a conventional oven, or 160°C for a fan forced oven (325-350F or gas mark 3-4). Grease the bottom and sides of a 23 cm springform pan/tin, and line the bottom with nonstick baking paper. Place the flour, desiccated coconut and butter into a food processor and mix until smooth. Pour the lime juice into mixture and blend again until the mixture forms a dough-like consistency. Roll out to about 4mm thick (about 1/4 inch).
2. Press into the base and sides of your prepared tin and line with foil, and bake for approximately 15 mins. Take out the foil.
3. Put the cream cheese, coconut cream and sugar into a food processor or you can mix with an electric beater. Mix until smooth, add the eggs and egg yolks one at a time, beat again until smooth and creamy and all eggs have been added to the mixture. Pour into the base and bake for approx. 45 Minutes or until it looks like it has set. Remove from the baking pan/tin and allow cooling completely. Top with mango and coconut, and serve.

Tips:

If you can't get hold of coconut cream, you can use coconut milk, but you will need to add an extra egg otherwise it won't set very well.

When buying Mangoes it is best to use your sense of smell, they should be fragrant, and have a tropical smell about them. Depending on which variety you have available will depend on what color they are; they are usually a pinky/red color and are soft but firm to the touch when ripe. Very soft or bruised mangoes should be avoided. Don't buy green mangoes as sometimes they don't ripen. If fresh mangoes are not available, use a tin of sliced mangoes.

2. Mixed Berry Cheesecake

Prep Time: 10 minutes
Cooking Time: 45 minutes
Servings: 5
Ingredients:
- 250g (2.1/2 cups biscuit crumbs) plain biscuits of your choice
- 100g (1/2 cup) melted butter
- 2 eggs
- 1 Tbsp. (15ml) sugar
- 1 tsp. (5ml) corn flour
- 3/4 cup milk
- 1.1/2 Tbsp. (23ml) boiling water
- 1 Tbsp. (15ml) gelatin
- 250g cream cheese at room
- 2/3 cup sour cream
- 85g (1/3 cup) superfine/caster sugar (extra)
- 6 oz. each of strawberries, blueberries and raspberries (or any berries of your choosing)
- 1/4 cup raspberry jam

Directions:
1. Prepare a 23cm springform cake pan/tin by greasing and lining with non-stick baking paper. Crush the biscuits in a food processor until they resemble fine breadcrumbs, add the melted butter and mix until combined. Put the crumbs in the prepared cake pan/tin and press evenly into the base. Freeze for approx. 30 mins.
2. Hull and chop the strawberries and mix with the blueberries and raspberries and put to one side. Do this very gently as we don't want to crush the raspberries.
3. Separate the egg yolks into a bowl and put the egg whites to one side. Add the superfine/caster sugar and corn flour and beat until pale and thick. Put the milk into a pan and heat until almost boiling, then add to the egg mixture very slowly, whisking all the time. Return the mixture to the pan and heat until it thickens stirring all the time. Once it has a custard consistency to it, remove from heat and put to one side covered to stop a skin forming.
4. Mix the gelatin with the water and stir until dissolved and lump free. Add to the custard mix by pouring through a warmed tea or coffee strainer (see hints and tips) and stir to mix through.
5. Put the cream cheese, sour cream and extra superfine/caster sugar into a separate bowl and beat until smooth and creamy, then fold into the custard mixture. Beat the egg whites until you reach stiff peaks and the gently fold into the custard mixture. Gently fold the berries through the mixture, pour over the base and place in the fridge until set – overnight works well with this one.
6. When the cheesecake is ready, decorate by heating the jam either in the microwave for about 30 seconds or in a small pan. Pour the jam through a small sieve to remove the seeds and spread over the top of the cheesecake and put back in the fridge for about 30 minutes for the jam to set. When you are ready, remove from the pan/tin and serve. (Always looks really good with some extra berries scattered on the plates and a sprig of mint, if available).

3. Passion fruit Cheesecake

Prep Time: 10 minutes
Cooking Time: 7 hours
Servings: 5
Ingredients:
- 250g (2.1/2 biscuit crumbs) shortbread biscuits
- 100g (1/2 cup) melted butter
- 500g cream cheese
- 175gm (3/4 cup) superfine/caster sugar
- 1/4 cup lemon juice
- 3 tsp (15ml) gelatin dissolved in 1/4 cup boiling water
- 1 cup heavy/double cream
- 2 x 170 gm tins passionfruit pulp

Directions:
1. Prepare a 23cm springform cake pan/tin by lightly greasing and covering the base with non-stick baking paper. Put the biscuits in a food processor and pulse until resembles breadcrumbs, pour in the melted butter and mix through. Press the biscuit mix into the bottom of the cake pan and put into the freezer for about 30 minutes to set.
2. Lightly whip the cream, then place the cream cheese and sugar into a separate bowl and beat with an electric beater until smooth, add the lemon juice and gelatin mixture, then gently mix in one of the 170g tins of passionfruit pulp and fold through the lightly whipped cream. Pour into the prepared tin and place in the fridge until set, usually between 6-8 hours. Decorate with the one tin of passionfruit pulp, and add a couple of chopped kiwi fruit (Chinese gooseberries) mixed into the passionfruit pulp and spoon over the top of the cheesecake.

4. Pineapple Cheesecake

Prep Time: 10 minutes
Cooking Time: 7 hours
Servings: 5
Ingredients:
- 250g (2.1/2 cups biscuit crumbs) biscuits, choice of biscuit
- 100g (1/2 cup) butter melted
- 250g cream cheese
- 1 x 395g tin condensed milk
- 75ml (1/3 cup) lemon juice
- 1 x 450g can crushed pineapple

Directions:
1. Prepare a 23cm springform pan/tin by greasing and covering the base with non-stick baking paper. Using a rolling pin or a food processor, crush the biscuits after placing them in a plastic bag that can be sealed. Melt the butter and mix with the biscuit crumbs, press into the base of the baking pan/tin and place in the freezer for about 30 mins.
2. Beat the cream cheese until smooth, gradually adding the condensed milk and the lemon juice. Drain the crushed pineapple, then add it and incorporate it into the cheese mixture. Pour into prepared pan/tin and place in the fridge for 6-8 hours or overnight to set. You could decorate with this slices of pineapple threaded onto a toothpick with a glace cherry. Another idea would be to peel and slice a fresh pineapple thinly and then cut out 'flower' shapes and scatter on the top of the cheesecake.

5. Raspberry Cheesecake

Time: 10 minutes
Cooking Time: 45 minutes
Servings: 5
Ingredients:
- 250g (2.1/2 biscuit crumbs) ginger biscuits
- 125g (1/2cup) butter, melted
- 2 tsp. (10ml) finely grated lemon zest
- 80g (1/4cup) raspberry jam, warmed
- 250g Raspberries
- 2 tsp. (10ml) gelatin
- 250g cream cheese, at room temperature
- 125g (1/2 cup) sugar
- 1 Tbsp. lemon juice
- 300ml thickened/heavy cream

Directions:
1. Grease and line a 23cm springform baking pan/tin with non-stick baking paper. Crush the biscuits until they look like fine breadcrumbs, add the butter and lemon zest, mix thoroughly and then press into the bottom and sides(if you like the biscuit base on the sides) of the baking pan/tin. Place in the freezer for about 30mins.
2. Add 2 Tbsp. water in a heatproof bowl over a pan of simmering water, add the gelatin and stir until completely dissolved (or just follow the instructions on the packet). While the gelatin is cooling, beat the cream cheese, sugar and lemon juice in a mixing bowl or if using a food processor, pulse until smooth, scraping down the sides of the bowl every few minutes so that you don't have any lumps at the end and beating again until smooth. Pour into prepared tin, refrigerate until set, and then decorate by sprinkling the raspberries over the top, and brush with the warmed jam.

6. Strawberry Cheesecake (with a few raspberries)

Prep Time: 10 minutes
Cooking Time: 70 minutes
Servings: 5
Ingredients:
- 250g (2.1/2 cups biscuit crumbs) plain biscuits
- 150g (3/4 cup) butter melted
- 500g cream cheese at room temperature
- 125g (1/2 cup) superfine/caster sugar
- Finely grated rind of 1 lemon
- 2 eggs
- 1/2 cup sour cream
- 500g fresh strawberries, hulled
- 200g raspberries

Directions:
1. Grease either 6 x 5cm deep x 8cm diameter baking pans/tins or a 23cm baking pan/tin. Line an oven tray with non-stick baking paper and place rings onto the tray (if using 23cm pan/tin you don't need to put it onto a baking tray at this stage). .Line the inside of the rings or pan with a narrow piece of the baking paper.
2. Crush the biscuits until they resemble breadcrumbs mix with the melted butter until combined. If making 6 small cheesecakes, divide the mixture evenly between the individual rings and press the mixture down onto the tray using a straight sided glass. If using the large pan/tin, you will be able to do this using your hands. Place in the freezer for about 30 minutes.
3. In the meantime, preheat the oven to about 160°C for a fan forced oven and 180°C for a conventional oven (325-350°F or gas mark 4).
4. Add cream cheese, sugar and the lemon ring into a bowl and beat until smooth. If you are using a food processor (and I do), pulse it until the mixture is the correct consistency, and please don't forget to scrape the sides down and add to the mixture and beat again or you will get a lumpy mixture.
5. Beat the eggs together in a separate bowl, and add to mixture in two lots (i.e. use half then beat, then the other half and then beat until the mixture is smooth). Fold in the sour cream.
6. Pour the mixture evenly over the six bases, or into the larger pan and bake the smaller ones for 30 minutes or the larger cake for about 60 minutes or until they are just set. Turn off the oven and leave the cheesecakes in the oven with the door open for an hour until cooled. Remove from the oven and when completely cooled cover with film or foil and put in the fridge.
7. Put 250g strawberries into a food processor and process until smooth then pour through a sieve or a colander lined with muslin or cheesecloth to remove any excess seeds, and stir icing sugar into this mixture and refrigerate until required. Chop the remaining strawberries into quarters.
8. Remove cheesecakes from their baking rings/pans and place onto individual plates or place a slice of cheesecake onto the plates if you have made one large one. Pour over strawberry juice, sprinkle with quartered strawberries and decorate with a sprig of mint.

7. New York Baked Cheesecake

Prep Time: 10 minutes
Cooking Time: 1 hour
Servings: 5
Ingredients:
- 100g (1/2 cup) melted butter
- 250g (2.1/2 cups biscuit crumbs) either Graham or Digestive biscuits
- 725g cream cheese at room temperature
- 1 can (14oz/395g) sweetened condensed milk
- 1 tsp (10ml) vanilla extract
- 2 eggs

Directions:
1. Prepare a 23 cm springform baking pan/tin by greasing and covering the base with non-stick baking paper. Preheat the oven to 150°C for a conventional oven 135°C for a fan forced oven, or 300°F gas mark 2 cool setting.
2. Make the cheesecake base by crushing the biscuits (easiest way is in a food processor) until they look like breadcrumbs, add the melted butter and stir until combined. Press into the base of the prepared tin and place in the freezer for about 30 mins.
3. Beat the cream cheese until light and fluffy in a mixing bowl, and gradually add the can of sweetened condensed milk, ensuring that it is beaten well and all mixed together. Beat well after each addition of the egg, then add the vanilla and beat once more.
4. Pour the cheese mixture onto the base and bake in the oven for about 1 hour, then turn the oven off, open the door and leave in the oven to cool for about 1 hour. Remove from the oven and allow to completely cool at room temperature. When cool, refrigerate for a few hours until firm.

8. Oreo Cheesecake

Prep Time: 10 minutes
Cooking Time: 40 minutes
Servings: 5
Ingredients:
- 1 (approx. 200g) packet Oreo biscuits crushed
- 100g (1/2 cup) butter, melted
- 600g cream cheese
- 1/2 cup double cream (heavy whipping cream)
- 1/4 cup milk
- 175g superfine/caster sugar
- 2 eggs
- 24 chopped Oreo biscuits

Directions:
1. Grease and line the base of a 23 cm springform baking pan with non-stick baking paper. Heat the oven to 160°C for a conventional oven, 145° for a fan forced oven, 325°F or Gas mark 3. Mix the crushed Oreo biscuits with the butter until combined and press into the base of the prepared pan/tin. Place in the freezer for about 30 mins.
2. Whip the cream cheese until smooth then beat in the sugar, milk and cream and mix until smooth. Beat the eggs lightly in a separate small bowl and then add to the cream mixture beating in one at a time until they have just combined. Fold the 24 chopped Oreo biscuits into the mixture. Pour the mixture onto the prepared base bake for approximately 35 to 40 minutes or until the center is almost set, then cool. Once cool, place in the fridge until you are ready to decorate.
3. You can decorate with mini Oreos if you want to. Just place them sideways into the mixture, leaving about half of the biscuit above the mixture. Otherwise you can decorate with whipped cream swirls and chopped chocolate, or just leave it plain, it will taste yummy whichever way you serve it!

9. Red Velvet cheesecake

Prep Time: 10 minutes
Cooking Time: 40 minutes
Servings: 5
Ingredients:
- 185g (approx. 1 cup) butter at room temperature
- 155g (3/4 cup) superfine/caster sugar
- 2 eggs
- 115g (3/4 cup) self-raising flour
- 40g (1/4 cup) plain flour
- 2 Tbsp (30ml) cocoa powder
- 1/4 tsp bicarbonate of soda
- 125ml (1/2 cup) buttermilk
- 2 Tbsp red food coloring
- White chocolate curls for decoration – see Guide to Chocolate

Filling:
- 250g cream cheese at room temperature
- 70g (1/3 cup) superfine/caster sugar
- 2 Tbsp. (30ml) lemon juice
- 2 Tbsp. (30ml) warm water
- 1.1/2 tsp gelatin

Cream cheese topping:
- 250g cream cheese at room temperature
- 60g butter at room temperature
- 80g confectioners/icing sugar
- 1/4 tsp vanilla extract

Directions:
1. Preheat the oven to 180°C for a conventional oven, (160°C for a fan assisted oven, Gas mark 4, moderate or 350°F)
2. Prepare a 23cm cake pan/tin by greasing and lining the bottom with nonstick baking paper.
3. Combine the butter and sugar and beat them until they are light and fluffy. Add the eggs one at a time, beating well after each addition. In a bowl, sift together the self-rising flour, regular flour, cocoa powder, and bicarbonate of soda. Stir the flour and buttermilk into the creamed butter and sugar alternately, and then add the red food coloring. Pour mixture into prepared pan/tin and bake for about 35-40mins. If a spear inserted into the cake comes out clean, the cake is done. Lay out on a wire rack to cool.
4. Slice the cake in half and level the top by trimming of any 'rounded' parts.

For the filling:
1. Beat the cream cheese, sugar and lemon juice with an electric beater or you can pulse in a food processor until combined, remembering to scrape down the sides and pulsing again so that there are no lumpy bits left in the mixture.

2. Once everything is well-combined, combine the gelatin according to the packet's directions. Once the gelatin has dissolved, add to the filling by pouring through a tea or coffee strainer that has been placed in hot water to warm ensuring no lumpy gelatin bits go into the mixture, and beat until it is all mixed together. Beat the cream to the soft peak stage and fold into the cream cheese mixture.
3. Using the same 23cm cake pan/tin, brush again with oil and line with plastic wrap (cling film, or saran wrap) ensuring that the wrap overhangs the sides. Return the cake base to the pan, with the base cut side up.
4. Spread the filling over the cake base, place the top of the cake on top and cover the top with plastic wrap and place in the fridge for at least 3 hours or preferably overnight to chill.

For the icing/frosting:
1. Beat the cream cheese, butter, sugar and vanilla in a bowl until light a creamy and the sugar crystals have completely dissolved.
2. Remove the cake from the springform tin, spread the top with the icing, and decorate with chocolate curls. Absolutely beautiful – enjoy.

10. Classic Cheesecake

Prep Time: 10 minutes
Cooking Time: 2 hours
Servings: 5
Ingredients:
For the crust
- 2 cups unroasted almonds
- 5 to 7 pitted dates
- 1 1/2 tbsp coconut or avocado oil
- 1/2tsp vanilla extract
- 1/2 tsp sea salt

For the filling
- 3 cups raw cashews (soaked and drained)
- 3/4 cup juice of lemon
- 2/3 cup melted coconut oil
- 3/4 coconut sugar
- 1 - 2 tsp vanilla extract
- Pinch of sea salt
- 1 cup berries of your choice

Directions:
1. Process almonds, dates, coconut oil, vanilla and salt in a food processor until mixture turns into dough. Press enough dough mixture into the pan and place in the freezer. Excess dough will be used for the second layer.
2. Blend all ingredients until a smooth, creamy texture is achieved. After adding the berries, pour the remaining mixture into the crust.
3. Then add the extra dough on top of the filling. Pour the remaining filling mixture and top with berries.
4. Place in the freezer for at least 2 hours. Then serve.

11. Coconut Cardamom Cheesecake

Prep Time: 10 minutes
Cooking Time: 5 hours
Servings: 5
Ingredients:
For the crust
- 1 cup raw almonds
- 2/3 cup pitted raisins or dates
- Dash of salt

For the Filling
- 1 cup ripe mango, diced
- 2/3 cup unroasted cashews
- 6 Tbsp. water
- 3 Tbsp. agave or maple syrup
- 1 1/2 tsp vanilla extract
- 1 tsp. fresh juice of lemon
- 1/2 - 1 tsp. cardamom powder
- 4 Tbsp. coconut butter, melted
- 7 Tbsp. coconut oil, melted

Directions:
1. Grind almonds by using a food processor and then add raisin and salt. Slowly add water and make sure that the mixture should loosely hold together when pressed by hand.
2. Combine all the ingredients for the filling except for the coconut butter and oil until it has a smooth texture. Then add the coconut butter and oil, and mix well.
3. Pour the filling into the crust. Place in the freezer for at least 5 hours.
4. Garnish the cheesecake with grated coconut and crushed nuts, and then serve.

12. Concorde Grape Cheesecake with Fig and Grape Puree

Prep Time: 10 minutes
Cooking Time: 40 minutes
Servings: 5
Ingredients:

For the crust
- 1 1/2 cups raw macadamia or almond nuts
- 2 tbsp agave or maple syrup
- 1/2 – 1 tsp vanilla extract
- Dash of sea salt

For the filling
- 2 cups fresh juice of Concorde grapes
- 3 cups raw cashews
- 1/2 cup + 4 tsp agave or maple syrup
- 4 tsp fresh juice of lemon
- 6 tbsp coconut oil, melted
- 2 tbsp sunflower lecithin
- For the topping
- 1/2 cup fresh juice of Concorde grapes
- 1/2 cup figs, dried and cut in halves
- 1 pitted date
- Chia seeds

Directions:
1. 1. Finely chop macadamia nuts in a food processor. Add the other ingredients until texture sticks together when pressed. After distributing the mixture into a pan, set the pan aside.
2. Place Concorde grape juice, cashews and agave in a blender. Mix together until smooth and creamy. Add coconut oil and lecithin and mix well.
3. Pour the mixture on to the prepared crust. Chill until the filling is firm.
4. Mix juice, figs, dates and chia seeds until puree are made.
5. Spread the puree before serving.

13. Cranberry Grape Cheesecake

Prep Time: 10 minutes
Cooking Time: 8 hours
Servings: 5
Ingredients:
For the crust
- 1 cup raw almonds
- 1/3 cup oat groats, rolled
- 3 Tbsp. maple or coconut sugar
- 1 Tbsp. maple syrup or agave nectar
- 1/2 tsp. vanilla extract
- 2 Tbsp. coconut oil, melted

For the filling
- 2 cups cranberries, fresh
- 1 1/2 cups raw cashews
- 3/4 cup fresh juice of grapes
- 1/3 cup maple syrup
- 2 Tbsp. fresh juice of lemon
- Stevia, to taste
- 5 Tbsp. coconut oil, melted
- 2 Tbsp. cacao butter, melted

For the topping
- 1 1/3 cup cranberries, fresh
- 1/2 cup chopped pitted dates
- 3 Tbsp. fresh juice of grapes or orange
- Orange zest

Directions:
1. Grind almonds into fine crumbs using a food processor. Add in the oats, sugar, syrup and vanilla and mix well. Then add coconut oil and mix to form a consistent texture. Press the mixture into the pan and then set aside.
2. Blend all ingredients for the filling except for coconut oil and cacao butter until the mixture is smooth. After that, combine all of the remaining ingredients well.
3. Spoon the prepared crust with the mixture. Refrigerate for at least 8 hours.
4. Prepare topping by blending all ingredients. Make sure chunks of fruits are still visible.
5. Spread the topping on the cheesecake before serving.

14. Double Chocolate Cherry Cheesecake

Prep Time: 10 minutes
Cooking Time: 55 minutes
Servings: 5
Ingredients:

For the crust
- 1 3/4 cups almond or hazelnuts
- 1/2 cup cacao nibs, raw
- Dash of sea salt
- 3/4 tsp. cherry extract, pure
- 1 Tbsp. raw cacao powder
- 3/4 cup pitted raisins or dates

For the filling
- 3 cups raw cashews, (soaked and drained)
- 1/3 cup raw agave or maple syrup
- 6 large, pitted dates
- 1/2 cup fresh juice of lemon
- 1/4 cup water
- 2 tsp. cherry extract, pure
- 1 cup melted coconut oil
- 3/4 cup cacao powder, unsweetened

For the topping
- Handful of frozen cherries (or berries)
- 1/4 cup raw agave or maple syrup
- Squeeze of fresh lemon juice
- Dash of cinnamon

Directions:
1. Add salt, almonds, and cacao nibs to a food processor. Mix well before adding the chocolate powder and cherry extract. When the mixture comes together when pushed by hand, add the raisins last. Place the pan with the mixture in the refrigerator.
2. In a blender, combine the cashews, agave, dates, lemon juice, and water until the mixture is smooth. Then incorporate cacao powder, coconut oil, and cherry essence. Mix thoroughly until the consistency is uniform.
3. Pour the mixture in the chilled crust and place in the freezer until filling has set.
4. Blend the cherries, agave, lemon juice and cinnamon until the mixture is smooth.
5. Spread or drizzle the topping on the cheesecake before serving.

15. Double Crusted Pumpkin Chocolate Cheesecake

Prep Time: 10 minutes
Cooking Time: 30 minutes
Servings: 5
Ingredients:
For the crust
Crust 1
- 1/2 cup almonds, raw
- 1/2 cup pecans, raw
- 8 large, pitted dates
- 1 tsp. powdered vanilla
- Pinch of salt
- Dash of cinnamon

Crust 2
- 3/4 cup dark agave nectar
- 1/3 cup melted coconut oil
- 3/4 cup cocoa powder, unsweetened

For the filling
- 1 cup homemade almond milk
- 1 cup dark agave nectar
- 2 Tbsp. lemon juice, fresh
- 3 cups raw cashews (soaked and drained)
- 3 cups shredded butternut squash
- 1 Tbsp. powdered Lucuma
- 2 Tbsp. powdered vanilla
- Pinch of sea salt
- Dash of turmeric powder
- 1 - 2 tsp. pumpkin pie spice
- 3 Tbsp. sunflower lecithin
- 1 cup melted coconut oil

Directions:
1. For the crust 1, grind all ingredients except for the date until texture is formed into fine crumbs. Then add the dates one at a time until the mixture clumps together. Press the mixture into a pan and then set aside.
2. For the crust 2, blend all ingredients until the texture is smooth. Spread half of the mixture on to the first crust. Place in the fridge to chill.
3. **For the filling,** add all ingredients listed except for the lecithin and coconut oil. Mix well until smooth and creamy. Then add the remaining ingredients, blend again until texture is consistent.
4. Pour filling mixture into the chilled crust. Add the remaining 2nd crust mixture and then create swirls.

5. After that, freeze it for the filling to become firm.
6. Dust cacao powder on top when served.

16. Key Lime Cheesecake with Coconut Cream Topping

Prep Time: 10 minutes
Cooking Time: 45 minutes
Servings: 5
Ingredients:
For the crust
- 1 cup almonds, raw
- 4 large pitted dates
- 2 Tbsp. coconut oil, organic
- Few drops of vanilla extract
- Pinch of sea salt

For the Filling
- 1 1/2 cup macadamia nuts, raw
- 1/2 cup homemade almond milk
- 1/2 cup lime juice, fresh
- 6 Tbsp. maple syrup or agave syrup
- 1/2-1 tsp. pure vanilla extract
- 6 tsp. melted coconut oil

For the topping
- 1 can coconut milk, unsweetened
- 1 - 2 tsp. vanilla extract
- 1 - 2 Tbsp. raw coconut sugar

Directions:
1. **For the crust,** mix all ingredients until the mixture forms fine crumbs. Place in the freezer to harden.
2. **For the filling,** combine all ingredients until mixture is smooth and creamy.
3. Pour mixture on the chilled crust and refrigerate until the filling sets.
4. **For the topping**, place canned coconut milk in the fridge, overnight.
5. Once the can is opened, scoop the thick cream layer and place in a mixer.
6. Add the vanilla and coconut sugar and whisk.
7. Top cheesecake with coconut cream and then serve.

17. Lemon Berry Swirl Cheesecake

Prep Time: 10 minutes
Cooking Time: 50 minutes
Servings: 5
Ingredients:
For the crust
- 1 1/2 cups raw almonds
- 2/3 cup pitted dates
- 1/4 cup coconut, shredded
- 1 tsp. vanilla extract

For the filling
- 3 cups unroasted cashews
- 3/4 cup lemon juice, fresh
- 2/3 cup agave or maple syrup
- Pinch of sea salt
- Lemon zest
- 1 cup coconut oil, melted
- 4 cups different berries

Directions:
For the crust
1. Grind all ingredients in a food processor except for the shredded coconut and vanilla until the texture is crumbly.
2. Add the remaining ingredients until the mixture sticks together like dough.
3. Press the mixture in a pan and set aside.

For the filling
1. Blend all ingredients except for coconut oil and berries until the mixture is smooth.
2. Then add 2/3 cup of coconut oil to the mixture and blend again.
3. Pour 1/2- 2/3 cup mixture in a separate bowl.
4. Add berries and 1/3 cup coconut oil to the remaining mixture in the blender and mix well until smooth and creamy.
5. Pour the berry mixture in the prepared crust.
6. Scoop a spoon of lemon mixture on top of the berry filling.
7. Using a stick, push the lemon mixture in the berry filling and create a swirling motion.
8. Place in the fridge until the filling is firm.
9. Garnish with frozen berries before serving.

18. Sweet Kale Cheesecake

Prep Time: 10 minutes
Cooking Time: 35 minutes
Servings: 5
Ingredients:
- 1 cup raw cashews nuts
- 1 ripe banana, mashed
- 3/4 – 1 cup kale
- 1/3 cup melted coconut oil
- 1/3 cup maple syrup or coconut nectar
- 2 1/2 Tbsps. fresh juice of lemon
- Pinch of sea salt

Directions:
1. Blend all ingredients until smooth and creamy mixture is achieved.
2. Pour mixture in a glass dish or molds and then spread evenly.
3. Put for at least five hours in the refrigerator.
4. Serve and enjoy!

19. Tiramisu with Vanilla Cream and Coffee Ladyfingers

Prep Time: 10 minutes
Cooking Time: 60 minutes
Servings: 5
Ingredients:
For the crust
- 1 cup gluten free oats, rolled or raw walnuts
- 1 cup pitted raisins or dates
- 2 Tbsp. pressed coffee

For the lady finger
- 1 cup oats, rolled
- 1 cup large, pitted dates
- Pinch of sea salt
- 1/2-1 tsp. vanilla extract
- 2 Tbsp. pressed coffee

For the filling
- 2 cups raw macadamia nuts or raw hazelnuts
- 1-2 cups water
- 1/4 cup melted coconut oil
- 3 Tbsp. coconut nectar or agave nectar
- 1/2-1 Tbsp. vanilla extract
- 3 tsp. soy or sunflower lecithin (optional)

Directions:
1. Grind oats or walnuts to form flour by using a food processor.
2. Add raisins and coffee and mix well.
3. Press mixture on the pan and place in the fridge.
4. Process oats to become flour using a food processor.
5. Add the rest of the ingredients of the lady finger until mixture sticks together.
6. Place lady finger mixture in a pan and dehydrate for 2 hours or place in an oven.
7. For the filling, blend all the ingredients until mixture is smooth and thick.
8. Pour half of the filling on the prepared crust.
9. Place lady finger on top to cover the filling.
10. Spread evenly the remaining filling on top.
11. Place in the fridge until mixture is firm.
12. Garnish with cacao powder before serving.

20. Triple Berry Swirl Cheesecake

Prep Time: 10 minutes
Cooking Time: 25 minutes
Servings: 5
Ingredients:

For the crust
- 1 cup of raw almond nuts
- 4 large, pitted dates

For the filling
- 1 ¼ cup homemade almond milk
- 1 ½ cups raw cashews
- 1/3 cup agave or maple syrup
- 1 - 2 tsp. pure vanilla extract
- ¼ cup cacao butter, melted
- 1 Tbsp. soy or sunflower lecithin
- Handful of raspberries, blackberries and blueberries

Directions:
1. **For the crust**, process nuts and dates in a food processor until the mixture clumps together. Then press evenly in a pan.
2. **For the filling,** blend almond milk, cashews, agave and vanilla extract until the mixture is smooth and creamy. Then add the cacao butter and lecithin, and mix well.
3. Pour a cup of mixture in a small bowl.
4. Add the mixed berries to the remaining filling mixture until the consistency is smooth.
5. Pour half of the berry filling on the crust.
6. Then pour evenly the white filling on top.
7. Repeat layering.
8. Using a chopstick or a butter knife, create a swirling motion on the filling.
9. Place in the fridge until it sets.
10. Top with berries or fresh fruits that you like.

21. Vanilla Chocolate Brownie Cheesecake with Strawberry Sauce

Prep Time: 10 minutes
Cooking Time: 35 minutes
Servings: 5
Ingredients:
For the crust
Date Nut Crust
- 1 cup raw walnuts
- 2/3 cup large, pitted dates

Chocolate Brownie Crust
- 1 cup raw almonds, sliced
- 1/2 cup raw walnuts or pecans
- 1 cup chopped, pitted dates
- 1/4 -1/3 cup cacao powder, unsweetened
- 1/2 - 1 tsp. pure vanilla
- Pinch of sea salt
- 2 tsp. water

For the filling
- 2 cups raw cashews
- 7 Tbsp. coconut milk or almond milk
- 8 Tbsp. coconut nectar or agave syrup
- 1-2 Tbsp. pure vanilla extract
- 4 tsp. fresh juice of lemon
- 1 vanilla bean seeds
- Pinch of sea salt
- 1/2 cup coconut oil, melted

For the sauce
- 2 cups fresh strawberries, chopped
- 3-4 large, pitted dates
- Fresh juice of lemon

Directions:
1. In making the crust, you have the option to make date nut crust or chocolate brownie crust.
2. Process all ingredients of the crust that you want to make until a dough texture is achieved. Press crust mixture into a pan and set aside.
3. For the filling, blend all ingredients except for the oil and vanilla bean until you get a mixture that is smooth.
4. After that, combine all of the remaining ingredients well.
5. Pour the filling in the prepared crust and chill until it has set.
6. For the strawberry sauce, blend all ingredients until smooth and creamy.
7. Spread the sauce on top of the cheesecake and then serve.

22. Vanilla Lemon Cheesecake

Prep Time: 10 minutes
Cooking Time: 40 minutes
Servings: 4
Ingredients:
For the crust
- 2 cups of raw walnuts
- 1 cup large dates
- 1/2 fine shredded coconut meat
- 1/4 cup ginger, finely chopped

For the filling
- 2 cups of soaked cashews, raw
- 1 whole lemon without skin and seeds
- 1/2 – 3/4 cup agave syrup or maple syrup
- 3/4 cup melted coconut oil
- 1 ripe, mashed banana
- 1/2 -1 tsp. pure vanilla extract

Directions:
1. Grind all the ingredients of the crust until the texture forms fine crumbs.
2. Then evenly press the crust mixture in a pan and set aside.
3. Blend all the ingredients of the filling until the texture is smooth and pour over the prepared crust.
4. Store for at least 4 hours in the refrigerator.
5. Top cheesecakes with desired fruits and other decorations before serving.

23. Chocolate Quark Cheesecake

Prep Time: 1 hr.
Cooking Time: 30 Minutes
Servings: 4
Ingredients:
Crust
- ½ cup sugar
- ⅛ tsp. salt
- 1 egg
- 1½ cups/180g all-purpose flour
- ¼ cup/30g cocoa powder
- 7 Tbsp. unsalted high-fat, softened
- ¾ tsp. baking powder

Filling
- 8½ Tbsp. unsalted butter
- 2 cups Quark, drained if necessary (see this page)
- ½ cup plus 2 Tbsp. granulated sugar
- 2 eggs
- 2 tsp. vanilla extract
- 1 Tbsp. cornstarch

Directions:
1. For crust: Beat together the butter & sugar till fluffy. Add the egg after scraping the sides.
2. Combine the baking powder, flour, cocoa powder, and salt in a different bowl. With the motor on, add the flour mixture into the butter mixture until well-combined. Remove the dough onto plastic wrap & form into a disk. It should be soft but not sticky. Wrap it up & refrigerate for 30 mins.
3. Divide the dough in 1/2 & form each piece into a disk. Wrap one disk in the plastic wrap and return it to the refrigerator.
4. Roll out the second disk between two pieces of plastic wrap until it is approximately 11 inches/28cm in diameter. Remove off the top piece of plastic wrap, and then invert the dough over a 9-inch/23cm springform pan and fit it gently into the pan, removing the plastic wrap as you go. The dough should come up the sides by about 1 inch/2.5cm. Trim any excess and use it to patch any imperfections or set it aside to combine with the remaining dough for the topping. Refrigerate the lined pan while you make the filling.
5. To make the filling: Heat the oven to 350°F/180°C. Melt the butter. Set aside to cool slightly. Place the Quark in a bowl & whisk in the sugar, either by hand or with an electric mixer. Beat in the eggs & then the cooled butter, vanilla extract, and cornstarch.
6. When the mixture is creamy and well combined, remove the crust from the refrigerator and pour the filling into the crust. Smooth the top. If necessary, using a knife, trim the sides of the cocoa crust so that it is even all the way around and about ¼ inch/6mm higher than the Quark filling. Reserve any trimmings.

7. Remove the reserved dough & briefly knead together with any reserved trimmings. Pluck off ½-inch/12mm pieces of the dough and scatter them evenly over the surface of the Quark filling. The pieces of cocoa dough won't sink, but rather will rest on top of the raw filling. Place in the oven & bake for 45-50 mins. The Quark filling will be browned in color and inflated.
8. Remove & let cool on a rack for 20 minutes. Run a thin knife around the pan's edge after 20 minutes to help the cake come loose. Let the ring cool completely before taking off.
9. A day after baking, the cake tastes best. It can be chilled when it has completely cooled and is lightly wrapped in plastic wrap. Serve refrigerated or at room temperature. The cake will keep nicely in the refrigerator for at least 3 days and up to 1 week.

24. Chocolate Cheesecake

Prep Time: 15 Minutes
Cooking Time: 1 hr. plus cooling time
Servings: 4
Ingredients:
For the Crust:
- 12 Oreo cookies, crushed, plus extra to serve
- 1 Tbsp. white sugar
- 2 Tbsp. unsalted butter, melted

For the Filling:
- 4 Tbsp. milk
- 1 cup semisweet chocolate chips
- ½ tsp. espresso powder
- 12 oz. cream cheese, softened
- 1/2 cup white sugar
- 2 large eggs
- ½ tsp. vanilla extract
- 1 Tbsp. flour

Directions:
1. Preheat the oven to 375F & slightly grease a 6"inch springform pan.
2. For the Crust: In a medium-sized bowl, combine the crushed Oreos, sugar & melted butter. Press the crumb mixture in pan & bake for 10 minutes. Remove & set aside to slightly cool.
3. Reduce the oven to 350°F.
4. For the filling: In a saucepan, combine the milk and chocolate chips and heat on low until the chocolate chips are melted. Remove from heat and add in the espresso powder. Set the mixture aside.
5. In a large bowl, beat together the cream cheese and sugar for about 2 minutes. Add in the eggs & beat again until well-combined. Finally, add in the vanilla extract and flour and beat until well-combined.
6. Pour batter onto the crust then bake for about 45 minutes or until a toothpick placed into the edge of the cake comes out clean.
7. Turn off the oven and, leave the door open several inches and leave to cool for about an hour.
8. Remove, cover and cool in the refrigerator for another hour or until ready to serve.
9. Top with crushed Oreos and serve.

25. Carrot Cake Cheesecake

Prep Time: 20 Minutes plus 5 hrs.
Cooking Time: 1 hr.
Servings: 4
Ingredients:
Cheesecake:
- 1 tsp. vanilla
- 3 eggs
- 1 Tbsp. flour
- 2 (8-oz.) blocks cream cheese, room temperature
- ¾ cup sugar

Carrot Cake:
- ¾ cup vegetable oil
- 1 tsp. vanilla
- 1 cup sugar
- 1 tsp. cinnamon
- 2 eggs
- 1 cup flour
- ½ cup flaked coconut
- 1 tsp. baking soda
- 1 dash salt
- ½ cup chopped walnuts
- 1 (8-oz.) can crushed pineapple, well drained with juice kept aside
- 1 cup grated carrot

Pineapple Cream Cheese Frosting:
- 1 ¾ cups powdered sugar
- 2 oz. cream cheese, softened
- ½ tsp. vanilla
- 1 Tbsp. butter, softened
- 1 Tbsp. reserved pineapple juice

Directions:
1. Preheat oven to 350F & grease a 9-inch springform pan.
2. Blend the cream cheese and sugar in a bowl. The flour, eggs, and vanilla are then well mixed. Place aside.
3. Combine the 3/4 cup vegetable oil, sugar, eggs, and vanilla in another big basin and whisk until smooth. After that, beat until smooth before adding the flour, baking soda, cinnamon, and salt. Fold in the chopped walnuts, coconut, shredded carrot, and crushed pineapple.
4. In the prepared pan, add 1 1/2 cups of the carrot cake batter. On top of the carrot cake batter, drop spoonfuls of the cream cheese batter. Put spoonfuls of carrot cake batter on top of the cream cheese batter after that. Continue by using the remaining batter.

5. Cook for 50 to 60 minutes. Take out and allow to cool for about an hour before removing the springform pan's sides. Place in the fridge for at least five hours.
6. Beat together all the frosting ingredients. Frost the cake when it is completely cold.

26. Fruit Cheesecake Pie

Prep Time: 30 Minutes
Cooking Time: 30 Minutes
Servings: 4
Ingredients:

Fruit Layer
- 3 cups fresh fruit (cherries, rhubarb, pineapple, etc.)
- 1 Tbsp. water
- 1 cup sugar
- 2 Tbsp. cornstarch
- 1 tsp. flavored gelatin, for color

Cheesecake Topping
- Two 3-oz. packages cream cheese, softened
- 2 eggs
- 1 Tbsp. lemon juice
- 6 Tbsp. sugar
- 1 cup sour cream or nondairy substitute

Directions:
1. Preheat oven to 350F.
2. Prepare the crust (reserving 2 Tbsps. of the mixture). Do not bake.
3. Prepare the fruit by cutting the rhubarb into ½-inch slices, pitting the cherries or peeling, coring, and cutting the pineapple into small (½ inch or less) tidbits.
4. In a 2-quart saucepan, mix together the selected fruit, the water, sugar, and cornstarch. (Eliminate the water if the fruit is very juicy.) Cook, stirring often over medium heat, until the mixture comes to a full boil. Remove from heat and add the gelatin (raspberry for rhubarb, cherry for cherry, and lemon for apple and pineapple). Pour the fruit mixture over prepared crust.
5. With a mixer, blend together the cream cheese, eggs, lemon juice, sugar, and sour cream. Pour over the fruit filling. Top with a sprinkling of the reserved crumb mix.
6. Bake for 25 to 30 minutes, or until the center appears set when shaken gently.
7. Cool and then refrigerate from 2 to 24 hours before serving.

27. Nutella Oreo Cheesecake

Prep Time: 15 Minutes
Cooking Time: 1 hour plus cooling time
Servings: 4
Ingredients:
For the Crust:
- 12 Oreo cookies, crushed, plus extra to serve
- 1 Tbsp. white sugar
- 2 Tbsp. unsalted butter, melted

For the Filling:
- 4 Tbsp. milk
- 1 cup Nutella
- ½ tsp. espresso powder
- 12 oz. cream cheese, softened
- 1/2 cup white sugar
- 2 large eggs
- ½ tsp. vanilla extract
- 1 Tbsp. flour

Directions:
1. Preheat the oven to 375F & slightly grease a 6"inch springform pan.
2. For the Crust: In a medium-sized bowl, combine the crushed Oreos, sugar & melted butter. Press the crumb mixture in pan & bake for 10 minutes. Remove & set aside to slightly cool.
3. Reduce the oven to 350°F.
4. For the Filling: In a saucepan, combine the milk and Nutella, and heat on low until the chocolate chips are melted. Add the espresso powder after removing from the heat. Set the mixture aside.
5. In a large bowl, beat together the cream cheese and sugar for about 2 minutes. Add in the eggs & beat again until well-combined. Finally, add in the vanilla extract and flour and beat until well-combined.
6. Spread batter over the crust, then bake for about 45 minutes, or until a toothpick inserted into the cake's edge comes out clean.
7. Turn off the oven and, leave the door open several inches and leave to cool for about an hour.
8. Remove, cover and cool in the refrigerator for another hour or until ready to serve.
9. Top with crushed Oreos and serve.
10. Enjoy!

28. Caramel Cheesecake

Prep Time: 4 hrs. 15 Minutes
Cooking Time: 1 hr. 5 Minutes
Servings: 4
Ingredients:
Crust:
- ⅓ cup margarine, melted
- ¼ tsp. ground cinnamon
- 1 ½ cups graham cracker crumbs

Filling:
- 2 tsp. vanilla extract
- 4 (8-oz.) packages cream cheese, softened
- ½ cup sour cream
- 5 large eggs
- 1 cup Dulce de Leche
- 1 ¼ cups white sugar

Directions:
1. Preheat oven to 475F & place a skillet with half an inch of water inside.
2. Combine the ingredients for crust in a bowl. Line a large pie pan with parchment paper and spread crust onto pan. Press firmly. Cover it with foil & keep it in the freezer until ready to use.
3. In a bowl, combine all the filling ingredients, excluding the eggs. Mix in eggs 1 at a time & beat until fully blended.
4. Remove the crust & pour in the filling, spreading it evenly. Place the pie pan into the heated skillet in the oven and bake for about 12 minutes.
5. Reduce the heat to 350°F. Continue to bake for about 50 minutes, or until the top of the cake is golden. Remove it from the oven & move the skillet onto a wire rack to cool.
6. Refrigerate for at least 4 hours.
7. Serve cold.

29. Berry-Ricotta Cheesecake

Prep Time: 1 hr.
Cooking Time: 1 hr.
Servings: 4
Ingredients:
- 1 1/2 cup graham cracker crumbs
- 6 Tbsp. butter (margarine)
- 1 1/2 cup granulated sugar
- 1 Tbsp. of granulated sugar
- 2 lemons
- 15 oz. ricotta cheese
- 16 oz. reduced-fat cream cheese (Neufchatel)
- 2 cups half-and-half
- 2 tsp. vanilla extract
- 3 Tbsp. cornstarch
- 1 tsp. almond extract
- 4 large eggs
- 1 Tbsp. confectioners' sugar
- 2 1/2 cups mixed berries

Directions:
1. Preheat the oven at 375 degrees Fahrenheit.
2. Cover with a heavy-duty foil the exterior part a nine-inch springform pan to prevent leakage. Spray the pan with cooking spray.
3. Combine in a medium bowl the cracker crumbs, 1 Tbsp. of granulated sugar and butter. Press the mixture firmly on the bottom of the springform pan.
4. Bake the crust for 8-10 minutes until the edge is browned. Let cool on wire rack. Reduce oven temperature to 325 degrees Fahrenheit.
5. Meanwhile, grate from lemon fruit one Tbsp. peel and squeeze out at least one-fourth cup of juice, set aside.
6. Beat in a bowl of a mixer the ricotta cheese and the reduced-fat cream cheese on high speed until smooth.
7. Beat in cornstarch, ¼ tsp. salt and 1 ½ cups of granulated sugar. Scrape the sides of the bowl with a rubber spatula; continue beating on low speed until fully blended.
8. Add half-and-half, almond extracts, and vanilla and beat on low speed, add the lemon juice and lemon peel. Beat in eggs until all ingredients are blended well.
9. Fill the crust with the batter and bake for one hour. Turn off oven & leave the cake stand in oven for one hour.
10. Loosen the edge of cake by running a knife. Cool in a pan rack for one hour before covering and placing in refrigerator for six hours until two days.
11. Spread berries on top of the cheesecake. Spread confectioner's sugar on the berries through a sieve.
12. Serve!

30. Banana Cream Cheesecake

Prep Time: 20 minutes
Cooking Time: 1 hr. 30 minutes
Servings: 4
Ingredients:
- ¼ cup margarine, melted
- ½ cup whipping cream
- 3 (8-oz.) packages cream cheese, softened
- ⅔ cup sugar
- 20 vanilla sandwich cookies
- 3 eggs
- 2 Tbsp. cornstarch
- ¾ cup mashed bananas
- 2 tsp. vanilla extract

Directions:
1. Preheat the oven to 350F.
2. Crush the cookies in either a food processor or blender. When they have turned to crumbs, add the melted butter. Place the mixture in a springform pan and press to entirely cover the bottom and up the sides of the pan. Refrigerate this while you prepare the filling.
3. Whip the cream cheese till smooth, & then add in sugar & corn starch. When the cheese mixture is well blended, add in the eggs one at a time.
4. When the eggs are incorporated, add the whipping cream, bananas, and vanilla, beating until well combined.
5. Pour into the springform pan & bake at 350°F for 15 minutes. Reduce the heat to 200°F and bake until the center of the cheesecake is set, about 1 hour and 15 minutes.
6. When the center is set, remove the cake from the oven. Pop the spring on the pan, but don't remove the sides until the cheesecake has cooled completely. When it is cool, transfer it to the refrigerator. Refrigerate for at least 4 hours before serving.
7. Serve with whipped cream and freshly sliced bananas.

31. Pistachio Cheesecake

Prep Time: 10 minutes
Cooking Time: 50 minutes
Servings: 3
Ingredients:
- 2 or 2.5 cups crushed digestive biscuits
- 2 cups castor sugar
- 6 Tbsp. melted butter
- ¼ tsp. salt
- 3 cups cream cheese
- 1 cup chopped pistachios
- 4 eggs
- ½ tsp. cinnamon powder
- 2 tsp. almond essence
- 1 cup sour cream
- 1 cup whipping cream
- ½ tsp. green food color

Directions:
1. Mix the crushed crumbs with the butter and sugar.
2. Lay this mixture on top of a greased baking dish. Firm it using a spatula and even it out.
3. Bake this crust in an oven for about 11 minutes at 350 degrees F. Let it cool.
4. In a bowl, combine cream cheese, castor sugar and whip it until it's fluffed up.
5. Add the eggs one by one and beat it again.
6. Add the chopped pistachios, food color, almond essence, cinnamon powder, whipping cream and sour cream and mix well.
7. Pour this cake batter on top of the crust and bake it for 90 minutes at 325 degrees F.
8. Let it sit on the rack for about 30 minutes before removing.

For the topping
1. Take a sauce pan and roast some thinly chopped pistachios on a medium flame.
2. Sprinkle these on top of the cake and serve.

32. Carrot Cheesecake

Prep Time: 10 minutes
Cooking Time: 40 minutes
Servings: 3
Ingredients:
- 2 cups digestive biscuit crumbs
- ¼ cup melted butter
- ½ cups pecan nuts
- 1 cup self-rising flour
- 1 tsp. baking powder
- ¾ tsp. baking soda
- 1 tsp. cinnamon powder
- ½ tsp. minced ginger
- Salt – to taste
- 2 eggs
- 2 cups castor sugar
- 1 ½ shredded carrots
- ¾ cup sour cream
- 1 ½ cup cream cheese
- 1 tsp. vanilla essence

Directions:
1. Mix the biscuit crumbs with butter and sugar.
2. Pour this mixture on a greased baking tray and even it out using your hands.
3. Refrigerate for 2 hours until firm.
4. In a bowl, combine the pecans, baking powder, baking soda, flour, ginger, cinnamon powder and salt and mix well.
5. Slide in the eggs one by one and beat the mixture using an electric mixer.
6. Now gently fold in the cream cheese and shredded carrots and bake for about 25 minutes at 325°F.
7. Let it sit for about 30 minutes on the rack to cool down.

For the topping:
1. Whisk together the sour cream, 3 Tbsp. sugar and vanilla essence and spread it on top of the cake.
2. Garnish with some pecans.

33. Chocolate Cupcakes With Pumpkin Cheesecake Filling

Prep Time: 15 Minutes
Cooking time: 25 Minutes
Servings: 2
Ingredients
Filling:
- 1 (8 oz.) package cream cheese, at room temperature
- 1/3 cup white sugar
- 1 egg
- 2 Tbsp. 100% pure pumpkin
- 6 drops yellow food coloring (optional)
- 3 drops red food coloring (optional)
- 1/8 tsp. salt
- 1/2 cup semisweet chocolate chips, or more to taste

Cake:
- 1 1/2 cups all-purpose flour
- 1 cup white sugar
- 1/4 cup unsweetened cocoa powder
- 1 tsp. baking soda
- 1/2 tsp. salt
- 1/3 cup vegetable oil
- 1 cup water
- 1 tsp. white vinegar
- 1 tsp. vanilla extract

Directions:
1. Set the oven to 175 degrees Celsius (350 degrees F). Line paper liners onto a muffin tin.
2. In a bowl, put salt, red food coloring, yellow food coloring, pumpkin, egg, 1/3 cup sugar, and cream cheese. Then beat with an electric mixer until and no lumps remain and combined thoroughly. Mix in chocolate chips.
3. In a large bowl, whisk together the 1/2 tsp. salt, baking soda, cocoa powder, 1 cup sugar and flour. Stir in the vanilla extract, vinegar, oil and water until the batter is blended well.
4. Add the batter into muffin cups until 1/2-full. Add 1 Tbsp. of cream cheese mixture on top. Scatter some chocolate chips on top.
5. Bake for about 25 minutes in the prepped oven until a toothpick comes out clean when inserted into the center.

34. Chocolate Peanut Butter Cheesecake Cups

Prep Time: 20 Minutes
Cooking time: 20 Minutes
Servings: 3
Ingredients:
Crust:
- 1 1/2 cups graham cracker crumbs
- 1/4 cup butter
- 4 Tbsp. white sugar
- 12 miniature peanut butter cups with chocolate coating (such as Reese's®), unwrapped

Filling:
- 2 (8 oz.) packages of softened cream cheese
- 1 cup white sugar
- 1/4 cup all-purpose flour
- 1 tsp. vanilla extract
- 2 eggs

Directions:
1. Set oven to 175° C (350° F) and start preheating. Set paper liners in a muffin tin.
2. Combine sugar, butter, and graham cracker crumbs in a bowl until the crumbs are moistened. Press the mixture into the bottom of every paper liner to make a crust. Put a peanut butter cup into the center of each crust.
3. Using a handheld electric mixer, whisk the cream cheese until fluffy. Put in vanilla extract, flour, and sugar; whisk thoroughly. One at a time, add the eggs, whisking well after each addition. Spread the cheese mixture over the peanut butter cups and graham cracker crusts using a spoon.
4. Put into the preheated oven and bake for 20 minutes, or till the filling is set. Let cheesecake cups cool completely.

35. Double Caramel Pecan Cheesecake Bars

Prep Time: 15 Minutes
Cooking time: 40 minutes
Servings: 3
Ingredients:
- 1 1/2 cups Nabisco Graham Cracker Crumbs
- 1 cup coarsely chopped Planters Pecans, divided
- 2 Tbsp. granulated sugar
- 1/4 cup butter, melted
- 4 (8 oz.) packages Philadelphia Cream Cheese, softened
- 1 cup firmly packed brown sugar
- 2 Tbsp. flour
- 1/2 cup Breakstone's or Knudsen Sour Cream
- 1 Tbsp. vanilla
- 3 eggs
- 1 (14 oz.) bag Kraft Caramels, divided
- 2 Tbsp. water, divided

Directions:
1. Preheat the oven to 350 ° F. Line foil on baking pan, 13x9-inch in size, with foil ends overhanging the pan sides. Combine butter, granulated sugar, a half cup of pecans and graham crumbs; firmly pat onto bottom of prepped pan. Bake for 10 minutes.
2. Use an electric mixer to whip the brown sugar, flour and cream cheese in a big bowl till thoroughly incorporated. Put in the vanilla and sour cream; combine thoroughly. Put in eggs, one by one, whipping at low speed after each addition just till incorporated. Put 3 dozens of caramels in microwave- safe bowl. Put in a Tbsp. of water. Microwave for a minute on high till the caramels fully melt once mixed. Put into the cream cheese batter; mix till thoroughly incorporated. Pour this over the crust.
3. Bake till the middle is nearly set, about 40 minutes. Scatter the leftover half cup of pecans on top. Cool fully. Chill for no less than 4 hours.
4. Put the rest of the caramels in microwave-safe bowl. Put leftover 1 Tbsp. of water. Microwave for a minute on high, till the caramels are fully melted once mixed. Sprinkle on top of cheesecake; allow to rest till firm. Take dessert out of pan using foil as handle prior to slicing to make bars and serve. Keep leftovers refrigerated.

36. Easy Sour Cream Cheesecake

Prep Time: 20 Minutes
Cooking time: 1hour 10 Minutes
Servings: 3
Ingredients:
- 1 (9 inch) prepared shortbread pie crust
- 2 (8 oz.) packages cream cheese
- 1 cup white sugar
- 2 eggs
- 2 tsp. vanilla extract
- 1 cup sour cream

Directions:
1. Preheat the oven to 165 degrees C (325 degrees F).
2. Mix the sugar and cream cheese together. Put in the eggs, one at a time; blend well. Put in the sour cream and vanilla. Add to the shortbread crust.
3. Bake in preheated oven till the cake jiggles evenly across top when being shaken gently or for 60-70 minutes. Slide the knife round the outside edge but keep the cake in pan. Allow it to cool down on the counter, then put into the fridge. Take out of the pan once chilled totally, then serve.

37. Easy Strawberry Cheesecake

Prep Time: 30 Minutes
Cooking time: 40 minutes
Servings: 3
Ingredients
- 3 cups digestive biscuits, crushed
- 12 Tbsp. unsalted butter
- 14 oz. cream cheese, softened
- 11 oz. mascarpone cheese
- 5/8 cup white sugar
- 1 1/4 cups heavy whipping cream
- 2 cups strawberries, hulled and halved, plus more for garnish

Directions:
1. For easier cutting and serving, line a large pie dish with parchment paper.
2. In a bowl, combine the melted butter and crushed biscuits. Press the mixture into the prepared dish and chill in the fridge for 30 minutes.
3. Mix together sugar, mascarpone cheese, and cream cheese in a bowl until well incorporated. Use an electric mixer to beat cream in a chilled metal or metal bowl until it can form soft peaks. Add to the cream cheese mixture by folding. Fold the remaining strawberries into the cream cheese mixture after setting aside a few for garnish.
4. Scoop the mixture onto the chilled biscuit base and use the back of a spoon to smooth out the top. Garnish with reserved strawberries. Refrigerate for 1 hour before serving.

38. Fig Hazelnut Cheesecake With Honey Bourbon Drizzle

Prep Time: 45 Minutes
Cooking time: 1hours
Servings: 3
Ingredients:
- 24 vanilla sandwich cookies with filling
- 4 Tbsp. butter, softened
- 8 oz. dried figs, roughly chopped, divided
- 1 1/2 cups roughly chopped toasted hazelnuts, divided
- 3 (8 oz.) packages cream cheese, softened
- 1 1/2 cups white sugar
- 1 1/2 Tbsp. all-purpose flour
- 2/3 cup sour cream
- 1/2 cup buttermilk
- 1 tsp. vanilla extract
- 1 tsp. hazelnut liqueur
- 4 eggs
- 1/4 cup honey
- 2 Tbsp. bourbon

Directions:
1. Warm up the oven to 140°C or 285°F. Wrap the bottom of a 9-inch springform pan with aluminum foil, then snap the plate into the ring. Using butter, coat the inner sides of the pan.
2. In a food processor, process the vanilla cookies to make a total of about 2 cups of crumbs. Put the crumbs into a bowl and then add butter, using a fork to blend. Press the vanilla cookie crumb mixture into the bottom of the pan. Top the crust with 1 cup of hazelnuts and 1/2 of the figs.
3. In a large bowl, take the cream cheese and beat with an electric mixer on low speed for about five minutes, scraping the sides of the bowl as you go. In another bowl, sift the flour and sugar together and then add to the cream cheese mixture. Add buttermilk, sour cream, hazelnut liqueur, and vanilla extract, beating thoroughly. On low speed mix, add 1 egg at a time until the yolks disappear. Pour the batter into the previously prepared pan.
4. Without opening the door of the preheated oven, bake for 60 minutes. Turn off the heat, but keep the cheesecake inside for an additional hour to let residual heat set it. Slightly open the oven door after 1 hour and then let the cheesecake cool in the oven for another 30 minutes. Take out the cheesecake and let it cool for another hour or so at room temperature.
5. Chill the cheesecake in the refrigerator for 1 hour. Unhook the pan clasp, slowly remove the ring, but make sure that the sides of the cake are not touched. Place the cheesecake in the freezer with or without cover for 8 hours or overnight. Take the cheesecake out of the freezer an hour before serving.
6. To prepare the topping before serving, place honey in a microwave-safe container and heat slightly. Mix in the bourbon. On the center and around the edge of the cheesecake, arrange the hazelnuts carefully. Sprinkle the honey-bourbon mixture on top of the cheesecake.

39. Five Star Cheesecake

Prep Time: 30 Minutes
Cooking time: 1hours15 Minutes
Servings: 4
Ingredients:
- 1/2 cup graham cracker crumbs
- 3 (8 oz.) packages cream cheese
- 7/8 cup white sugar
- 1/2 cup heavy cream
- 2 Tbsp. sour cream
- 1/4 cup half-and-half
- 1 1/2 tsp. vanilla extract
- 4 eggs

Directions:
1. Set the oven to 190°C (or 375°F) and start preheating. Use foil to wrap the outside of an 8" springform pan. Coat the inside of pan with a generous amount of butter, then add graham cracker crumbs on top; shake off the excess.
2. Beat sugar and cream cheese over low speed until smoothened in a big bowl. Beat in half-and-half, sour cream and heavy cream. Beat in eggs, one by one, and vanilla. Transfer the filling onto the wrapped pan. Using aluminum foil, wrap underneath the pan to avoid water from leaking in.
3. Transfer the cheesecake into a water bath. Bake for 1 1/4 hours in the prepared oven until the filling is set. Let it cool and refrigerate. Serve chilled.

40. Frosted Cream Cheese Brownies

Prep Time: 20 Minutes
Cooking time: 30 Minutes
Servings: 4
Ingredients:
- 1 package fudge brownie mix (13x9-inch pan size)
- 1/2 cup white baking chips

Filling:
- 3 oz. cream cheese, softened
- 2 Tbsp. butter, softened
- 1/4 cup sugar
- 1 large egg
- 1 Tbsp. all-purpose flour
- 1/2 tsp. orange extract

Frosting:
- 1 oz. unsweetened chocolate
- 1 oz. semisweet chocolate
- 2 Tbsp. butter
- 1 cup confectioners' sugar
- 2 to 3 Tbsp. whole milk

Directions:
1. Follow the package directions to prepare brownies f, then fold in the white chips. Spread a half of the batter in a greased 9"x13" baking pan.
2. Beat together sugar, butter and cream cheese in a small bowl until smooth. Beat in orange extract, flour and egg.
3. Mix the batter with the cream cheese mixture carefully. Drop the leftover brownie batter by spoonfuls on top of the cream cheese layer. Use a knife to slice through the batter to swirl.
4. Bake at 350 degrees until a toothpick comes out almost clean after inserting into the center, for 30 to 35 minutes. Allow to cool on a wire rack.
5. To create the frosting, in a microwave-safe bowl, melt the butter and chocolate. Then, mix until smooth. Allow to cool a little, then stir in enough milk and confectioners' sugar to get spreading consistency. Frost brownies.

41. Berry-topped Cheesecake

Prep Time: 30 Minutes
Cooking Time: 4 hours 55 minutes
Servings: 4
Ingredients:
- 2 Tbsp. sliced almonds, toasted
- 1½ cups small pretzel twists (2 oz.)
- ⅓ cup water
- 3 Tbsp. Butter
- 1 envelope unflavored gelatin
- ½ tsp. almond extract
- ¼ cup confectioners' sugar
- 8 oz. reduced-fat sour cream
- 12 oz. reduced-fat cream cheese, softened
- 1 cup fresh blackberries or blueberries
- 1 cup quartered or halved fresh strawberries
- 4 oz .light whipped dessert topping, frozen, thawed

Directions:
1. Mix almonds and pretzels in a food processor; cover and blend until crushed finely. Add the butter; cover and blend until incorporated. Press the pretzel mixture into an 8- or 9-inch springform pan's bottom—Bake from 8 to 10 minutes or until light brown. Let cool on a wire rack.
2. In a small saucepan, add the water; sprinkle gelatin on top (do not stir). Let sit for 5 minutes to soften. Cook and stir on low heat till the gelatin is dissolved; put aside to slightly cool down.
3. Add the almond extract, confectioners' sugar, sour cream, and cream cheese in a large bowl; use an electric mixer to beat on medium speed until it becomes smooth.
4. Spread evenly 1/2 of the filling on cooled crust. Place half of the blackberries and half of the strawberries on top. On top of the berries, spread the remaining cream cheese mixture. The cheesecake should be covered and chilled for 4 to 24 hours or until it has set.
5. To loosen, run a sharp, long knife around cheesecake's edge; take off the side of the pan. Slice cheesecake into wedges. Garnish each portion with some of the leftover blackberries and strawberries.

42. Best Ever Cheesecake

Prep Time: 30 Minutes
Cooking time: 40 minutes
Servings: 4
Ingredients:
- 1 cup sifted all-purpose flour
- 1/4 cup white sugar
- 1 tsp. lemon zest
- 1/2 cup butter
- 1 egg yolk, beaten
- 1/4 tsp. vanilla extract
- 20 oz. cream cheese
- 1/8 tsp. vanilla extract
- 1/2 tsp. lemon zest
- 1 1/2 Tbsp. all-purpose flour
- 1/8 tsp. salt
- 5/8 cup white sugar
- 2 eggs
- 1 egg yolk
- 2 Tbsp. heavy whipping cream

Directions:
1. Dough Crust: Mix 1 tsp. grated lemon peel, 1/4 cup sugar, and 1 cup flour; add in margarine/butter till it looks like coarse crumbs. Mix in 1/4 tsp. vanilla and beaten egg yolk. Pat 1/3 dough onto bottom of 1 9-in. springform pan that has the sides removed. Bake it for 6 minutes at 205°C/400°F. Cool. Butter pan sides; attach to the bottom. Evenly pat leftover dough on sides to 2-in. height.
2. Filling: Preheat an oven to 260°C/500°F. To soften the cream cheese, beat till fluffy. Add 1/2 tsp. grated lemon peel and 1/8 tsp. vanilla.
3. Mix leftover sugar, 1/8 tsp. salt, and 1 1/2 Tbsp. flour; blend it into the cream cheese mixture slowly. One by one, add egg yolk and eggs; beat well after each. Mix in heavy cream gently; put the batter in the prepped crust.
4. Bake it at 260°C/500°F till the crust's top edge is golden for 5-8 minutes. Lower the heat to 100°C/200°F and bake for 1 more hour. Take the cake out of the oven; cool for 3 hours minimum in a pan. Remove pan sides; serve.

43. Birthday Cake Cheesecake

Prep Time: 20 Minutes
Cooking time: 50 minutes
Servings: 4
Ingredients:
Crust
- 1 lb. sugar cookie dough

Filling
- 1½ lb. cream cheese softened
- 8 oz. sour cream
- 1½ cups sugar
- 4 large eggs, room temperature
- 2 tsp. vanilla extract
- ½ cup confetti sprinkles

Directions:
1. Prepare the oven to 350 degrees F, with the rack in the lower-middle position.
2. Fill a 9-inch springform pan with the sugar cookie batter. To make it even apply pressure.
3. Cook for about 10 minutes in the oven.
4. To create the filling, beat the softened cream cheese, sugar, sour cream, eggs, and vanilla together in a large mixing basin.
5. Stir in the confetti sprinkles.
6. Using a spatula, smooth the contents over the baked crust.
7. Place the springform pan in a bigger roasting pan after wrapping it in aluminum foil.
8. Boil water halfway up the springform pan in the roasting pan.
9. Preheat oven to 350°F and bake for 1 hour, or until the top is barely set. Allow cooling completely before releasing the spring and removing the ring by loosening the sides of the cheesecake from the pan with a knife.

44. Black Forest Cheesecake

Prep Time: 30 Minutes
Cooking time: 60 minutes
Servings: 4
Ingredients:
Crust
- 1½ cups dried chocolate cake or cookie crumbs
- 1 Tbsp. cocoa powder (if crumbs are not chocolate)
- 3 Tbsp. butter or margarine, melted

Cake
- 2, 8 oz. packages of cream cheese softened
- 1 cup cottage cheese
- 4 eggs
- 1 cup sugar
- ½ cup semisweet chocolate chips
- ½ cup maraschino cherries, drained and chopped

Directions:
1. Preheat oven to 375°.
2. Combine the crumbs, cocoa (if using), and butter. Pat into a 10" springform pan.
3. In a bowl, whip the cream cheese, cottage cheese, eggs, and sugar until well blended and smooth. Stir in the chocolate chips, and cherries. Pour gently into the crust. Bake for 35-40 mins/until the center is set.
4. When cool, put in the fridge overnight, before serving.

45. Blackberry Cheesecake Cups

Prep Time: 30 Minutes
Cooking time: 40 minutes
Servings: 4
Ingredients:
- 1 ½ cups miniature pretzels
- 3 Tbsp. butter, melted
- 2 Tbsp. sugar
- 1 cup heavy whipping cream
- 8 oz. cream cheese
- 1 tsp. vanilla extract
- ½ cup confectioners' sugar
- ½ cup white baking chips
- 1 ½ cups fresh blackberries, chopped
- 1/3 cup sugar

For serving
- Whipped cream
- Fresh blackberries

Directions:
Add the pretzels to a food processor and process until crushed.
1. Stir in the butter and 2 Tbsp. of sugar.
2. Pour the mixture into a glass jar with a lid.
3. Beat the cream with an electric mixer until you see stiff peaks forming.
4. In another bowl, beat the cream cheese, vanilla extract, and confectioners' sugar.
5. Stir in the whipped cream and baking chip.
6. Place the mixture on top of the pretzel mixture inside the jar.
7. Cover and refrigerate for 3 hours.
8. Add the blackberries and remaining sugar to a blender.
9. Process until pureed.
10. Add the blackberry puree to the glass jar.
11. Top with the additional whipped cream and blackberries.
12. Refrigerate for a few minutes or serve immediately.

46. Brown Sugar Amaretto Cheesecake

Prep Time: 30 Minutes
Cooking time: 45 minutes
Servings: 4
Ingredients:
Crust:
- ¼ cup butter, melted
- ½ cup graham crackers, crushed
- 1 cup Amaretti biscuits, crushed

Filling:
- ¼ cup Amaretto liqueur
- ½ cup light brown sugar
- 1 ½ pounds cream cheese
- 1 pinch salt
- 1 tsp. vanilla extract
- 2 egg yolks
- 2 eggs

Directions:
1. Crust: combine the biscuits, crackers, and butter in a container until well combined. Move to a 9-inch round cake pan and press it thoroughly on the bottom of the pan.
2. Filling: Combine all the ingredients in a container and mix thoroughly.
3. Pour the filling over the crust, preheat your oven and bake at 330F for about forty-five minutes or until set.
4. Let cool in the pan and serve, sliced.

47. Brownie Chocolate Chip Cheesecake

Prep Time: 30 Minutes
Cooking time: 55 minutes
Servings: 4
Ingredients:
- 1 (19.5 oz.) package Classic Traditional Fudge Brownies
- 3 (8 oz.) packages cream cheese, softened
- 1 (14 oz.) can Sweetened Condensed Milk
- 3 large eggs
- 2 Tbsp. vanilla extract
- 1/2 cup mini chocolate chips

Directions:
1. Preheat the oven to 350°F. Grease just the base of a springform pan, 9-inch in size. Prep brownie mix as instructed on packaging. Scatter smoothly in a prepped pan. Bake till set, for 35 minutes.
2. Whip the cream cheese in a big mixing bowl till fluffy. Slowly whip in sweetened condensed milk. Put vanilla and eggs; combine thoroughly. Mix chocolate chips in. Put to the prepped pan.
3. Lower oven heat to 300 ° F. Bake till set, for 50 minutes. Cool down. Chill well. Keep leftovers refrigerated with cover.

48. Butter Pecan Cheesecake

Prep Time: 30 Minutes
Cooking time: 54 minutes
Servings: 4
Ingredients:
- Butter (melted) 1/3 cup
- Pecans (finely chopped) ½ cup
- Sugar 1/3 cup
- Cracker crumbs 1 ½ cups

For Filling
- Pecans (finely chopped) 1 cup
- Eggs, large (lightly beaten) 3
- Butter flavoring ½ tsp.
- Vanilla extract 1 tsp.
- Sour cream 2 cups
- Sugar 1 ½ cups
- Cream cheese (softened) 1 cup

Directions:
1. To 325 degrees F, preheat the oven.
2. Take a large-sized bowl, gather the butter, pecans, sugar, and cracker crumbs. Put 1/3 cup of the mixture aside for topping.
3. Press the rest of the mixture onto the bottom of the greased springform pan (9 inches), 1 inch from the edges.
4. Put the springform pan onto the double thickness foil (heavy-duty) and wrap the foil around the pan securely.
5. Take a large-sized bowl, beat sugar and cream cheese until soft and smooth. Beat into it the butter flavoring, sour cream, and vanilla.
6. Put in the eggs and beat until combined well at low speed. Fold into the pecans. Pour into the crust. Sprinkle the saved mixture of crumbs. Put the springform pan onto a larger pan and pour hot water into the larger pan, almost 1 inch.
7. Bake for about 1 hour to 1 hour 30 minutes until the center becomes set. Take the springform out of the water bath. Transfer to the wire rack for 10 minutes to let it cool down.
8. Loosen the edges of the pan with a knife and refrigerate for 1 more hour. Refrigerate for the night, and cover when it completely cools down. Remove the sides of the pan.

49. Butterfinger Cheesecake

Prep Time: 30 Minutes
Cooking time: 30 minutes
Servings: 4
Ingredients:
- 1 1/2 (8 oz.) packages cream cheese
- 2 (8 oz.) whipped topping, creamy
- 1 (9 inches) prepared graham cracker crust
- 10 (2.1 oz.) bars crispy peanut butter candy, chocolate-covered

Directions:
1. In a bowl, combine cream cheese and 1 1/2 containers whipped topping together, then fold in the crushed candy. Pour into graham cracker crust. Spread the leftover whipped topping over it.
2. Refrigerate the cheesecake in the fridge for a minimum of 2 hours, until set.

50. Candy Bar Cheesecake

Prep Time: 30 Minutes
Cooking time: 45 minutes
Servings: 4
Ingredients:
- 1 lb. Cream Cheese
- 3/4 cup Brown Sugar
- 1/2 cup half and half
- 2 Eggs
- 1/2 cup Sour Cream
- 1 Tbsp. Vanilla
- 1/4 cup Flour
- 1/8 cup cocoa powder
- 1/4 cup chopped Reese's peanut butter cups
- 1/4 cup toffee pieces
- 1/4 cup Oreo pieces

Crust:
- 1 cup Oreo crumbs
- 1/4 cup brown sugar
- 1 tsp. salt
- 6 Tbsp. melted butter

Directions:
1. Make the cheesecake batter by creaming the sugar and cream cheese in a mixer. Beat until the mix is super light and smooth. Scrape down the bowl multiple times to make sure all of the cream cheese is blended in with the sugar.
2. Add the half and half and eggs slowly while the mixer is running. Stop occasionally to scrape down the bowl again to prevent lumps from forming; it is crucial to do this step slowly and also, at the same time, not to overmix the batter. Over mixing the eggs at this step will cause your cheesecake to crack later on when it is baking. Go slow and scrape the bowl, and you'll be okay!
3. After that, pour the sour cream and vanilla into the mixer all at once. Mix on low until the batter is just combined again, making sure not to over mix.
4. Add both flour and cocoa powder and stir briefly to incorporate.
5. Add the candy to the batter and fold it together.
6. Set the cheesecake batter aside for now while you make the crust.
7. Mix the salt, graham cracker crumbs, and melted butter sugar. Stir with a rubber spatula, or just use your hands to mix until the crust is fully combined and will hold its shape if you squeeze it together in your hand.
8. Press the crust into an 8" round springform pan. Pour the batter on the top of the crust.
9. Wrap the bottom of the pan in aluminum foil and then place the pan into a larger pan or casserole dish. Fill the larger pan with water about 3/4 of the way up the sides of the cheesecake pan.

10. Place the cheesecake in a 325°F and bake for about an hour. Touch the center of the cheesecake to test if it is done- the center should be slightly firm and not look liquid or shake when you touch it.
11. Let the cheesecake cool completely in the fridge before removing it from the pan. Serve cold.

51. Candy Cane Cheesecake

Prep Time: 30 Minutes
Cooking time: 56 minutes
Servings: 4
Ingredients:
- 3 Tbsp. white sugar
- 1 cup chocolate cookie crumbs
- 1/4 cup butter, melted
- 4 (8 oz.) packages cream cheese, softened
- 2 Tbsp. all-purpose flour
- 1/4 tsp. salt
- 1 3/4 cups white sugar
- 1/2 cup sour cream
- 2 1/2 tsp. vanilla extract, divided
- 3 eggs
- 1/2 tsp. peppermint extract
- 2 dashes of red food coloring
- 1/2 cup crushed peppermint candies

Directions:
1. Prepare the oven by preheating to 400°F (200°C). Prepare a 9-inch springform pan that is lightly greased.
2. In a bowl, mix 3 Tbsp. of sugar and cookie crumbs. Then drizzle melted butter in the mixture while whisking until equally moistened. And press the mixture at the bottom of the pan.
3. Place in the preheated oven and bake for 10 minutes until set; then take it out to cool. Lower the oven's temperature to 300°F (150°C).
4. In a big bowl, mix salt, flour, and cream cheese. Use an electric hand mixer and beat on low speed until fluffy and smooth. Put in 1 1/2 tsp. vanilla, sour cream, and 1 3/4 cups sugar and whisk until combined. Mix in eggs, one at a time, pausing and scraping the downsides of the bowl between every egg.
5. Split the mixture equally in two separate bowls. In a bowl, mix in 1 tsp. vanilla. Add the red food coloring mix and peppermint extract to the other bowl and blend until you achieve a reddish-pink color. If extra colour is required, add it. Up until all the the filling has been used, alternate layers of 1 cup of the white and pink on the chilled crust.
6. Bake for 60 to 70 minutes, or until the filling is set, in the preheated oven. The middle will shake slightly once the pan is shaken and the edges will be puffed slightly.
7. Dust the crushed candies equally over cheesecake and cautiously press on the top. Let it cool on a rack at room temperature. Then cover loosely and keep in the refrigerator overnight before serving.

52. Red Velvet Cheesecake

Prep Time: 30 Minutes
Cooking time: 58 minutes
Servings: 4
Ingredients:
- 2, 8 oz. packs of cream cheese, soft
- ½ cup of white sugar
- 1 tsp. of pure vanilla
- 2 eggs
- 2 oz. of semisweet chocolate, melted
- 1 Tbsp. of red food coloring
- 1, 6 oz. chocolate crumb crust

Directions:
1. Preheat the oven to 350 degrees.
2. Add the cream cheese into a bowl, white sugar and pure vanilla. Until thoroughly combined, beat with an electric mixer. Add in the eggs and continue to beat until mixed.
3. Add 1 cup of the batter into a bowl. Add in the melted semisweet chocolate and red food coloring. Stir well to mix.
4. Pour into the chocolate crumb crust. Top off with the remaining filling.
5. Place into the oven to bake for 40 minutes or until set.
6. Remove and set aside to cool completely. Cover and place into the fridge to chill for 3 hours.

53. Pina Colada Cheesecake

Prep Time: 30 Minutes
Cooking time: 1 hr. 15 minutes
Servings: 4
Ingredients:
- 6 Tbsp. of butter, melted
- 1 ¾ cups of graham cracker crumbs
- ¾ cup of pecans, toasted and chopped
- 1 Tbsp. of white sugar
- 3, 8 oz. packs of cream cheese, soft
- ½ cup of white sugar
- 5 eggs
- 1, 8 oz. can of pineapple, crushed
- 1 cup of cream of coconut
- 1 cup of sour cream
- 1/3 cup of light rum
- 4 tsp. of coconut extract
- Whipped cream, for garnish
- Coconut, toasted and for garnish

Ingredients for the glaze:
- 1 Tbsp. of cornstarch
- 1 Tbsp. of water
- 1, 8 oz. can of pineapple, crushed
- ¼ cup of white sugar
- 2 Tbsp. of lemon juice

Directions:
1. Preheat the oven to 325 degrees. Grease a 9 inch springform pan.
2. In a bowl, add in the melted butter, graham cracker crumbs, toasted pecans and white sugar. Stir well to mix. Press into the greased springform pan.
3. In a separate bowl, add in the soft cream cheese and ½ cup of white sugar. Beat with an electric mixer until fluffy in consistency. Add in the eggs, crushed pineapple, coconut cream, sour cream, rum and coconut extract. Continue to beat until mixed.
4. Pour the filling over the crust in the springform pan.
5. Place into the oven to bake for 1 hour and 15 minutes or until the cheesecake is set. Remove and set aside to cool completely.
6. In a bowl, add in the cornstarch and 1 Tbsp. of water. Whisk until smooth in consistency.
7. In a saucepan set over medium heat, add in the crushed pineapple, ¼ cup of white sugar and lemon juice. Add in the cornstarch mix. Stir well to mix. Cook for 5 minutes or until thick in consistency. Remove and set aside to cool completely.
8. Spread the glaze over the top of the cheesecake.
9. Cover and set into the fridge to chill for 8 hours.

10. Slice and serve.

54. Triple Chocolate Cheesecake

Prep **Time**: 30 Minutes
Cooking time: 1 hour 10 minutes
Servings: 4
Ingredients for the crust:
- 24 Oreo cookies, crushed
- ¼ cup of butter, melted

Ingredients for the filling:
- 2 lb. of cream cheese, soft
- 1 ½ cups of powdered sugar
- 3 Tbsp. of powdered cocoa
- 4 eggs
- 10 oz. of bittersweet chocolate, chopped

Ingredients for the topping:
- ¾ cup of heavy whipping cream
- 6 oz. of bittersweet chocolate, chopped
- 1 Tbsp. of white sugar

Directions:
1. Set the oven's temperature to 350. Make a 9-inch springform pan greased.
2. In a food processor, add in the Oreo cookies and melted butter. Pulse until moist. Press into the bottom of the springform pan.
3. Place the crust into the oven to bake for 7 minutes. Remove and set aside to cool completely.
4. Prepare the filling. In a bowl, add in the 10 oz. of chocolate. Microwave for 1 minute or until melted. Add in the cream cheese, white sugar, powdered cocoa and eggs. Beat with an electric mixer until smooth in consistency.
5. Pour over the crust.
6. Place into the oven to bake for 1 hour or until the top is set. Remove and set aside to cool completely. Cover and set into the fridge to chill for 8 hours.
7. Get the topping ready. Add the heavy whipping cream, chopped chocolate, and white sugar to a saucepan over low heat. Stir well until melted. Remove from heat and set aside to cool for 10 minutes. Pour over the cheesecake.
8. Garnish with chocolate curls and serve.

55. Cinnamon Roll Cheesecake

Prep Time: 30 Minutes
Cooking time: 1 hr. 30 minutes
Servings: 4
Ingredients:

For the crust:
- 1 ½ cups of Nilla wafer crumbs
- 4 Tbsp. of white sugar
- 1 tsp. of powdered cinnamon
- 5 Tbsp. of butter

For the cheesecake:
- 3, 8 oz. packs of cream cheese, soft
- 1 cup of white sugar
- 3 Tbsp. of all-purpose flour
- 4 eggs
- 1 cup of sour cream
- 2 tsp. of pure vanilla
- 2 tsp. of powdered cinnamon

For the filling:
- 2 cups of light brown sugar
- 5 Tbsp. of powdered cinnamon
- ¾ cup of all-purpose flour
- 12 Tbsp. of butter, melted

For the icing:
- 2 Tbsp. of cream cheese
- 6 Tbsp. of butter, soft
- ½ tsp. of pure vanilla
- 1 ½ cups of powdered sugar
- 4 to 5 Tbsp. of whole milk

Directions:
1. Preheat the oven to 325 degrees F.
2. Prepare the crust. In a bowl, add in the Nilla wafer crumbs, white sugar, powdered cinnamon and butter. Stir well until evenly mixed. Press into the bottom of a 9 inch springform pan. Place into the oven to bake for 10 minutes. Remove and set aside to cool.
3. Wrap the outside of the springform pan with aluminum foil. Set aside.
4. Lower the temperature of the oven to 300 degrees.
5. Prepare the filling and cheesecake. Add the cream cheese into a bowl, white sugar and all-purpose flour. Stir well until mixed. Add in the eggs, sour cream, pure vanilla and powdered cinnamon. Beat with an electric mixer on the lowest setting until mixed. Set aside.
6. In a separate bowl, add in the light brown sugar, powdered cinnamon, melted butter and all-purpose flour. Whisk well until mixed. Sprinkle over the bottom of the crust.

7. Spread 1/3 of the filling over the crumble mix. Repeat these layers until the cheesecake and the filling have been used. Sprinkle the remaining cinnamon mix over the top.
8. Insert a roasting pan into the springform pan.. Fill the outside of the springform pan with water halfway.
9. Place into the oven to bake for 1 hour and 20 minutes. Turn off the oven. Allow the cheesecake to rest in the oven for 30 minutes. Open the door slightly and continue to rest for 5 minutes. Remove and set aside to cool completely. Cover and set into the fridge to chill completely.
10. Prepare the icing. Add the cream cheese into a bowl, soft butter, pure vanilla, whole milk and powdered sugar. Beat with an electric mixer until smooth in consistency. Spread over the top of the cheesecake.
11. Slice and serve.

56. Classic Strawberry Cheesecake

Prep Time: 30 Minutes
Cooking time: 1 hr. 10 minutes
Servings: 4
Ingredients:

For the cheesecake:
- 3, 8 oz. packs of cream cheese, soft
- 1 cup of white sugar
- 3 eggs
- ¼ cup of sour cream
- 1 tsp. of pure vanilla
- 1 tsp. of lemon zest
- Strawberries, thinly sliced and for garnish

For the crust:
- 15 graham crackers, crushed
- 5 Tbsp. of butter, melted
- 2 Tbsp. of white sugar
- Dash of salt

For the sauce:
- 1 cup of strawberry preserves
- 2 tsp. of lemon juice

Directions:

1. Preheat the oven to 325 degrees F. Grease a 9 inch springform pan with cooking spray.
2. Prepare the cheesecake. Add the cream cheese into a bowl and white sugar. Beat with an electric mixer until smooth in consistency. Add in the eggs, sour cream, pure vanilla and lemon zest. Continue to beat until mixed.
3. Prepare the crust. In a bowl, add in the graham cracker crumbs, white sugar, melted butter and salt. Stir well to mix. Press into the bottom of the springform pan. Pour the cheesecake mix over the top of the crust.
4. Place into the oven to bake for 1 hour and 10 minutes or until the center is set. Turn off the oven. Allow the cheesecake to cool for 1 hour in the oven.
5. Cover and place into the fridge to chill for 4 hours.
6. Prepare the glaze. In a saucepan set over medium heat, add in the strawberry preserves and lemon juice. Whisk until smooth in consistency. Allow to come to a simmer. Remove from heat and set aside to cool.
7. Place the strawberries over the top of the cheesecake. Brush the glaze over the strawberries.
8. Cover and set back into the fridge to chill for 1 hour.
9. Slice and serve.

57. Pumpkin Cheesecake Bars

Prep Time: 30 Minutes
Cooking time: 45 minutes
Servings: 4
Ingredients:
For the crust:
- ¾ cup of crushed chocolate graham crackers
- 4 Tbsp. of butter, melted

For the filling:
- 2, 8 oz. packs of cream cheese, soft
- 1 cup of white sugar
- ¾ cup of pureed pumpkin
- 2 tsp. of pure vanilla
- 3 Tbsp. of all-purpose flour
- 1 ½ tsp. of pumpkin spice
- ¼ tsp. of salt
- 2 eggs, beaten

Directions:
1. Preheat the oven to 350 degrees. In a baking dish, add in a sheet of parchment paper.
2. Prepare the crust. In a food processor, add in the chocolate graham crackers and melted butter. Pulse until mixed. Press into the bottom of the baking dish. Place into the oven to bake for 8 minutes. Remove and set aside.
3. Prepare the filling. Add the cream cheese into a bowl. Beat with an electric mixer for 30 seconds or until creamy in consistency. Add in the white sugar, pureed pumpkin, pure vanilla, all-purpose flour, pumpkin spice, salt and beaten eggs. Continue to beat until mixed.
4. Pour the filling over the crust.
5. Place into the oven to bake for 35 to 38 minutes. Remove and set aside to cool completely. Cover and place into the fridge to chill for 2 to 4 hours.
6. Slice and serve.

58. Reese's Cheesecake

Prep Time: 30 Minutes
Cooking time: 60 minutes
Servings: 4
Ingredients:
or the crust:
- 20 Nutter butters
- 6 Tbsp. of butter, melted

For the cheesecake:
- 22 Reese's peanut butter cups, evenly divided
- 3, 8 oz. packs of cream cheese, soft
- ¾ cup of white sugar
- 3 eggs
- 1 cup of cream peanut butter, evenly divided
- ¼ cup of sour cream
- 1 tsp. of pure vanilla
- Reese's pieces, for topping

Directions:
1. Preheat the oven to 350 degrees. Wrap a 9 inch springform pan in two sheets of aluminum foil.
2. Prepare the crust. In a food processor, add in the nutter butters and melted butter. Pulse well until mixed. Press this mix into the bottom of the springform pan.
3. Add a layer of 16 Reese's cups over the top of the crust.
4. Prepare the filling. Add the cream cheese into a bowl and white sugar. Beat with an electric mixer until smooth in consistency. Add in the eggs, ¾ cup of the creamy peanut butter, sour cream and pure vanilla. Continue to beat until mixed. Pour over the Reese's cups in the pan.
5. Place the springform pan into a roasting pan filled with 2 inches of water.
6. Place into the oven to bake for 1 hour. Turn off the oven and open the door. Allow the cheesecake to rest for 1 hour. Cover and place into the fridge to chill for 5 hours.
7. Drizzle the remaining peanut butter over the cheesecake. Decorate with the remaining Reese's cups and Reese's pieces.
8. Slice and serve.

59. Caramel Cheesecake Bars

Prep Time: 10 Minutes
Cooking time: 55 minutes
Servings: 3
Ingredients:
For the crust:
- 2 ¼ cups of ground graham crackers
- 2 Tbsp. of white sugar
- ¼ tsp. of powdered cinnamon
- 10 Tbsp. of butter, melted

For the filling:
- 3, 8 oz. packs of cream cheese
- 1 cup of white sugar
- 3 eggs
- ½ cup of dulce de leche
- 2 tsp. of pure vanilla

For the caramel topping:
- 2/3 cup of dulce de leche
- 2 to 3 Tbsp. of heavy whipping cream
- 2 to 3 Tbsp. of caramel sauce

Directions:
1. Preheat the oven to 350 degrees. Grease a baking dish with cooking spray.
2. Prepare the crust. In a bowl, add in the ground graham crackers, white sugar, powdered cinnamon and melted butter. Stir well to mix. Press into the bottom of the baking dish. Place into the oven to bake for 10 minutes or until golden. Remove and set aside to cool completely.
3. Prepare the filling. In a separate bowl, add in the cream cheese, white sugar, eggs, dulce de leche and pure vanilla. Beat with an electric mixer until smooth in consistency. Pour over the crust in the baking dish.
4. Place into the oven to bake for 35 minutes or until set. Remove and cool completely.
5. Prepare the topping. In a bowl, add in the dulce de leche, heavy whipping cream and caramel sauce. Beat with an electric mixer until smooth in consistency.
6. Pour the caramel sauce over the cake.
7. Slice and serve.

60. Eggnog Cheesecake

Prep Time: 10 Minutes
Cooking time: 45 minutes
Servings: 3
Ingredients:
- 12 oz. of gingersnaps, ground
- ¼ cup of white sugar
- ¼ cup of melted butter
- 32 oz. of low fat cream cheese
- 4 eggs
- 2 cups of eggnog, evenly divided
- 2 cups of powdered sugar
- 2 Tbsp. of all-purpose flour
- 1 cup of heavy whipping cream
- Grated nutmeg, for garnish

Directions:
1. In a bowl, add in the ground gingersnaps, white sugar and melted butter. Stir well to mix. Press into the bottom of a 10 inch springform pan.
2. Add the cream cheese into a bowl. Beat with an electric mixer until smooth in consistency. Add in the eggs, 1 ½ cups of eggnog, powdered sugar and all-purpose flour. Continue to beat until smooth. Pour over the crust in the pan.
3. Place into the oven to bake for 1 hour at 325 degrees F. Turn off the oven. Allow the cheesecake to rest in the oven for 1 hour. Cover and place into the fridge to chill for 8 hours.
4. In a bowl, add in the heavy whipping cream. Beat with an electric mixer until peaks begin to form on the surface. Add in the remaining ½ cup of eggnog. Fold to gently incorporate.
5. Spread over the top of the cheesecake.
6. Slice and serve.

61. Lemon Bar Cheesecake

Prep Time: 10 Minutes
Cooking time: 60 minutes
Servings: 3
Ingredients:
- 2 cups of all-purpose flour
- ½ cup of powdered sugar
- ¼ tsp. of salt
- ½ cup of butter, cold and cut into cubes
- 2 egg yolks
- 1 to 2 Tbsp. of ice water
- 4, 8 oz. packs of cream cheese, soft
- 1 cup of white sugar
- 4 eggs
- 2 tsp. of pure vanilla
- 2 cups of lemon curd, evenly divided
- Candied lemon slices, for garnish

Directions:
1. In a food processor, add in the all-purpose flour, powdered sugar and dash of salt. Pulse until evenly blended. Add in the cold butter and continue to pulse until crumbly in consistency.
2. Add in the egg yolks and ice water. Continue to pulse until mixed.
3. Wrap the dough in a sheet of plastic wrap. Cover and set into the fridge to chill for 4 hours.
4. Roll the dough into a 14 inch sized circle on a flat surface. Place into a 9 inch springform pan. Cover and place into the fridge to chill for 30 minutes.
5. Preheat the oven to 325 degrees F.
6. Add the cream cheese into a bowl, 1 cup of white sugar, eggs and pure vanilla. Beat with an electric mixer until smooth in consistency.
7. Pour 2/3 of the filling over the crust. Add 1 cup of the lemon curd. Swirl around with a knife. Pour the remaining filling over the top.
8. Place into the oven to bake for 1 hour and 10 minutes or until the center is set. Remove from the oven and set aside to cool completely. Cover and chill for 8 hours.
9. Spoon the remaining cup of lemon curd over the cheesecake.
10. Top off with the candied lemon slices. Slice and serve.

62. Lemon Cheesecake

Prep Time: 10 minutes
Cooking Time: 35 minutes
Servings: 8

Ingredients:

For crust:
- 2 Tbsp. coconut oil, melted
- 2 Tbsp. swerve
- ¾ cup almond flour
- Pinch of salt

For filling:
- 2 Tbsp. heavy whipping cream
- 2 large eggs
- 1 tsp. lemon extract
- 1 tsp. lemon zest
- 4 Tbsp. fresh lemon juice
- 2/3 cup Swerve
- 1 lb. cream cheese, softened

Directions:
1. Grease a 7-inch springform pan with butter and line with parchment paper. Set aside.
2. In a bowl, combine together all the crust ingredients and pour into the prepared pan and spread evenly then place in the refrigerator for 15 minutes.
3. In a large mixing bowl, beat the cream cheese using a hand mixer until smooth.
4. Add swerve, lemon extract, lemon zest, and lemon juice and beat again until just combined.
5. Add eggs and heavy whipping cream and beat until well combined.
6. Pour the filling mixture over the crust and spread evenly. Cover the springform pan with foil.
7. Pour 1 cup of water into the instant pot then place a trivet in the pot.
8. Put the cake pan onto the trivet.
9. Seal instant pot with lid and select manual high pressure for 35 minutes.
10. Allow to release pressure naturally then open the lid.
11. Remove cake pan from the pot and let it cool completely.
12. Place in the refrigerator for 3-4 hours.
13. Serve chilled and enjoy.

63. Vanilla Cheesecake

Prep Time: 10 minutes
Cooking Time: 20 minutes
Servings: 8

Ingredients:
- 8 oz. cream cheese
- 2 eggs
- 1 tsp. vanilla
- 2/3 cup Swerve
- 1 cup strawberries, sliced

Directions:
1. Grease a springform pan with butter and line with parchment paper. Set aside.
2. Add cream cheese in a large bowl and beat using a hand mixer until smooth.
3. Add vanilla and swerve and blend until well incorporated.
4. Add eggs one at a time and blend until well combined.
5. Pour the batter into the prepared pan. Cover the pan tightly with foil.
6. Pour 1 cup of water into the instant pot then place a trivet in the pot.
7. Place cake pan on top of the trivet.
8. Seal instant pot with lid and select manual high pressure for 20 minutes.
9. Allow to release pressure naturally for 10 minutes then release using the quick release method.
10. Open the lid carefully. Remove cake pan from the pot and let it cool completely.
11. Once the cake is completely cool then arrange strawberry slices on top of the cake.
12. Cover cake with plastic wrap and place in refrigerator overnight.
13. Serve chilled and enjoy.

64. Chocolate Cheesecake

Prep Time: 10 minutes
Cooking Time: 35 minutes
Servings: 6

Ingredients:
- 16 oz. cream cheese
- 2 large eggs
- 4 Tbsp. unsweetened cocoa powder
- 2 Tbsp. heavy whipping cream
- ½ tsp. vanilla
- 2 tsp. coconut flour
- ½ cup Swerve

For topping:
- 2 tsp. swerve
- ½ cup sour cream

Directions:
1. Grease a springform pan with butter and line with parchment paper. Set aside.
2. Add cream cheese, cocoa powder, whipping cream, vanilla, coconut flour, and swerve to the large bowl and mix until well combined using a hand mixer.
3. Add eggs one at a time and mix until well combined.
4. Pour cheesecake batter into the prepared pan.
5. Pour 1 ½ cups of water into the instant pot then place a trivet in the pot.
6. Put the cake pan onto the trivet.
7. Seal the pot with lid and cook on manual high pressure for 35 minutes.
8. Allow to release pressure naturally then open the lid. Remove cake pan from the pot and let it cool completely.
9. Mix together the topping ingredients and spread on top of the cake.
10. Place cake in the refrigerator for 3-4 hours.
11. Slice and serve.

65. Delicious Chocó Cheesecake

Prep Time: 10 minutes
Cooking Time: 15 minutes
Servings: 8

Ingredients:
- 2 eggs
- 2 tsp. vanilla
- 1/4 cup sour cream
- 1/2 cup peanut flour
- 3/4 cup Swerve
- 16 oz. cream cheese
- 1 Tbsp. coconut oil
- 1/4 cup unsweetened chocolate chips
- 2 cups of water

Directions:
1. In a large bowl, beat cream cheese and swerve until smooth.
2. Gradually fold in vanilla, sour cream, and peanut flour.
3. Add eggs one at a time and fold well to combine.
4. Spray a 4-inch springform pan with cooking spray.
5. Pour the batter into the prepared pan and cover the pan with foil.
6. Pour 1 ½ cups of water into the instant pot then place a trivet in the pot.
7. Place the pan on top of the trivet.
8. Cover the instant pot with the lid and cook for 15 minutes on manual high pressure.
9. Allow to release pressure naturally then open the lid.
10. Remove cake pan from the pot and let it cool completely.
11. In a microwave safe bowl add coconut oil and chocolate chips and microwave for 30 seconds. Stir well.
12. Drizzle melted chocolate over the cheesecake and place in the refrigerator for 1-2 hours.
13. Serve chilled and enjoy.

66. Almond Cheesecake

Prep Time: 10 minutes
Cooking Time: 12 minutes
Servings: 6
Ingredients:

For crust:
- 3/4 cup almond flour
- 1 tsp. swerve
- 2 Tbsp. butter, melted

For cake:
- 2 eggs
- 1/4 cup sour cream
- 1 tsp. vanilla
- 1/4 tsp. liquid stevia
- 8 oz. cream cheese, softened

Directions:
1. Grease a 7-inch springform pan with butter, and line it with parchment paper.
2. In a bowl, combine together almond flour, butter, and swerve. Transfer the crust mixture into the prepared pan and spread evenly.
3. In another bowl, beat together the liquid stevia and cream cheese until smooth.
4. Add egg one at a time. Add the sour cream and vanilla and beat until smooth.
5. Pour the cheese mixture on top of the crust and spread evenly. Cover the dish with foil.
6. Pour 2 cups of water into the instant pot and place trivet in the pot.
7. Place the baking pan on top of the trivet.
8. Cover the instant pot with the lid and cook for 12 minutes on manual high pressure.
9. Allow to release pressure naturally then open the lid.
10. Remove cake pan from the pot and let it cool completely.
11. Slice and serve.

67. Ricotta Lemon Cheesecake

Prep Time: 10 minutes
Cooking Time: 30 minutes
Servings: 6
Ingredients:
- 2 eggs
- 1 lemon zest
- 1/3 cup ricotta cheese
- 1/4 cup Truvia
- 8 oz. cream cheese
- 1/2 tsp. lemon extract
- 1 lemon juice

Directions:
1. Add all the ingredients except the eggs into the mixing bowl and, using hand mixer, blend well until there are no lumps.
2. Add eggs and beat until well combined.
3. Pour the batter into a 6-inch springform pan and cover with foil.
4. Pour 2 cups of water into the instant pot and place the trivet into the pot.
5. Put the cake pan onto the trivet.
6. Seal the pot with lid and cook on high pressure for 30 minutes.
7. Allow to release pressure naturally then open the lid.
8. Remove the cake pan from the pot and let it cool completely.
9. Place in the refrigerator for 5-6 hours.
10. Serve and enjoy.

68. Vanilla Cheesecake

Prep Time: 10 minutes
Cooking Time: 20 minutes
Servings: 8
Ingredients:
- 8 oz. cream cheese
- 2 eggs
- 1 tsp. vanilla
- 2/3 cup Swerve
- 1 cup strawberries, sliced

Directions:
1. Grease a springform pan with butter and line with parchment paper. Set aside.
2. Add cream cheese in a large bowl and beat using a hand mixer until smooth.
3. Add vanilla and Swerve, and blend until well incorporated.
4. Add eggs one at a time and blend until well combined.
5. Pour the batter into the prepared pan. Cover the pan tightly with foil.
6. Add a trivet to the instant pot after adding 1 cup of water..
7. Put the cake pan onto the trivet.
8. Seal instant pot with lid and select manual high pressure for 20 minutes.
9. After 10 minutes of natural pressure release, use the quick release technique to relieve the pressure.
10. Open the lid carefully. Remove cake pan from the pot and let it cool completely.
11. Once the cake is completely cool, arrange strawberry slices on top.
12. Cover the cake with plastic wrap and place in the refrigerator overnight.
13. Serve chilled and enjoy.

69. Lemon Cheesecake in Mugs

Prep Time: 10 minutes
Cooking Time: 10 minutes
Servings: 3
Ingredients:
- 2 eggs
- 1 cup cream cheese
- ¼ cup heavy cream
- 1 tsp. Swerve
- 1 tsp. lemon extract
- 2 tsp. fresh lemon juice

Directions:
1. Add all the ingredients to a large bowl and mix until well combined.
2. Pour the batter into 3 heat-safe mugs and set aside.
3. Pour 2 cups of water into the Instant Pot and put a trivet in the pot.
4. Place the mugs on top of the trivet.
5. Seal the pot with lid and cook on high pressure for 10 minutes.
6. When finished, release pressure using quick release method and open the lid.
7. Let it cool down then refrigerate and chill before serving..

70. Blueberry Cheesecake

Prep Time: 10 minutes
Cooking Time: 30 minutes
Servings: 8
Ingredients:
- 4 eggs
- ½ cup heavy whipping cream
- 1 cup blueberry (plus for decoration)
- 1 cup erythritol
- 16 oz. cream cheese
- ¼ cup of coconut oil
- ½ cup almond flour
- 1 Tbsp. erythritol

Directions:
1. Line a 7-inch springform pan with parchment paper and set aside.
2. In a bowl, combine almond flour, coconut oil, and 1 Tbsp. erythritol.
3. Press the almond flour mixture into the bottom of the springform pan.
4. Wash and dry the blueberries. Grind the berries with a blender until mashed.
5. Combine heavy cream, 1 cup of erythritol, and cream cheese in a large bowl and whisk to combine.
6. Add eggs slowly and stir until well combined.
7. Add blueberries and fold in well.
8. Pour the cream cheese mixture into the pan over the crust.
9. Place a trivet inside the Instant Pot and add 1 cup of water.
10. Cover cake pan with foil and place on top of the trivet.
11. Cover the pot with a lid and cook for 30 minutes on manual.
12. When finished, allow pressure to release naturally, and then open the lid.
13. Remove the cake pan from the pot and let it cool completely.
14. Place in refrigerator for 4–5 hours.
15. Decorate the cake with blueberries on top.
16. Slice and serve.

71. Pumpkin Cheesecake

Prep Time: 10 minutes
Cooking Time: 83 minutes
Servings: 10
Ingredients:
For crust:
- ⅓ cup butter, melted
- 2 ½ Tbsp. erythritol
- 1⅓ cups almond flour

For filling:
- 1 tsp. vanilla extract
- ½ tsp. cinnamon
- 1 tsp. pumpkin pie spice
- 2 Tbsp. heavy cream
- 2 eggs
- 1 cup erythritol
- ⅔ cup pumpkin purée
- 16 oz. cream cheese, softened and cubed

Directions:
1. Line a springform cake pan with parchment paper and set aside.
2. In a medium bowl, mix together all ingredients for the crust until crumbly.
3. Add the crust mixture to the prepared pan and spread evenly. Press it down with hands.
4. Add all ingredients for the filling to a food processor and process until well combined.
5. Pour the filling mixture into the pan over the crust. Cover the pan with foil.
6. Place a trivet inside the Instant Pot and add 1 ½ cups of water.
7. Place the pan on top of the trivet in the Instant Pot.
8. Seal the pot with lid and cook on manual setting on high pressure for 58 minutes.
9. When finished, allow pressure to release naturally for 25 minutes, then release using the quick release method. Open the lid.
10. Remove pan from the pot and let it cool completely.
11. Place in refrigerator for 10–12 hours or until firm
12. Slice and serve.

72. Matcha Cheesecake

Prep Time: 10 minutes
Cooking Time: 35 minutes
Servings: 6
Ingredients:
- 2 eggs
- 1 Tbsp. matcha powder
- 16 oz. cream cheese
- 2 tsp. coconut flour
- ½ cup Swerve
- 2 Tbsp. heavy whipping cream
- ½ tsp. vanilla extract

Directions:
1. Spray a 7-inch springform pan with cooking spray and set aside.
2. Pour 1½ cups of water into the Instant Pot and put a trivet in the pot.
3. In a mixing bowl, add cream cheese, matcha powder, whipping cream, vanilla, coconut flour, and Swerve, and beat using a hand mixer until smooth.
4. Add eggs one at a time, beating after each, and mix well.
5. Pour the batter into the prepared pan and place pan on top of the trivet.
6. Seal the pot with lid and cook on high pressure for 35 minutes.
7. When finished, allow pressure to release naturally and then open the lid.
8. Remove the pan from the pot and let it cool completely.
9. Place in the refrigerator for 3–4 hours.
10. Slice and serve.

73. Classic Pound Cake

Prep Time: 10 minutes
Cooking Time: 55 minutes
Servings: 10
Ingredients:
- 4 eggs
- 1/2 cup sour cream
- 1 tsp. vanilla
- 1 cup monk fruit sweetener
- 1/4 cup cream cheese
- 1/4 cup butter
- 1 tsp. baking powder
- 1 Tbsp. coconut flour
- 1 cup almond flour

Directions:
1. Preheat the oven to 350 F.
2. Grease a 9-inch cake pan and set aside.
3. In a mixing bowl, mix together almond flour, baking powder, and coconut flour.
4. In a separate bowl, add cream cheese and butter and microwave for 30 seconds. Stir well and microwave for 3o seconds more.
5. Stir in sour cream, vanilla, and sweetener. Mix to combined.
6. Pour cream cheese mixture into the almond flour mixture and stir until well combined.
7. Add eggs in batter one by one and stir until well combined.
8. Fill the prepared cake pan with batter. Bake cake for 55 minutes.
9. Allow the cake to cool completely.
10. Slice and serve.

74. Moist Carrot Cake

Prep Time: 10 minutes
Cooking Time: 30 minutes
Servings: 10
Ingredients:
- 4 eggs
- 2 cups grated carrots
- 2 tsp. baking powder
- 1/2 tsp. xanthan gum
- 1/2 tsp. nutmeg
- 2 tsp. cinnamon
- 2 Tbsp. coconut flour
- 2 cups almond flour
- 2 tsp. vanilla
- 3/4 cup Swerve
- 3/4 cup butter
- Pinch of salt

Directions:
1. Preheat the oven to 350 F.
2. Grease the cake pan and set aside.
3. In a mixing bowl, beat butter and sweetener until light and fluffy. Add vanilla and eggs one by one and beat well.
4. In a separate bowl, mix together almond flour, baking powder, xanthan gum, nutmeg, cinnamon, coconut flour, and salt.
5. Stir the butter and egg mixture with the almond flour mixture until just combined.
6. Add grated carrots and stir well.
7. Fill the prepared cake pan with the batter, and bake for 25 to 30 minutes.
8. Allow the cake to cool completely.
9. Slice and serve.

75. Gooey & Rich Butter Cake

Prep Time: 10 minutes
Cooking Time: 45 minutes
Servings: 15
Ingredients:

For crust:
- 1 egg
- 2 cups almond flour
- 1/2 tsp. vanilla
- 1/2 cup butter, melted
- 2 tsp. baking powder
- 2 Tbsp. whey protein powder
- 1/2 cup Swerve
- Pinch of salt

For filling:
- 2 eggs
- 1/2 tsp. vanilla
- 3/4 cup Swerve
- 1/2 cup butter, softened
- 8 oz. cream cheese, softened

Directions:
1. Preheat the oven to 325 F.
2. Grease a 9*13 cake pan and set aside.
3. In a mixing bowl, mix together almond flour, baking powder, protein powder, sweetener, and salt.
4. Add egg, vanilla, and butter and stir until well combined.
5. Pour almond flour mixture into the prepared pan and spread well and press down.
6. For filling: In a separate bowl, beat butter and cream cheese until smooth. Add sweetener and beat until combined.
7. Add vanilla and eggs and beat until smooth.
8. Pour the filling over the crust and bake for 35-45 minutes.
9. Allow the cake to cool completely.
10. Slice and serve.

76. Lemon Pound Cake

Prep Time: 10 minutes
Cooking Time: 60 minutes
Servings: 16
Ingredients:
- 6 eggs
- 2 egg yolks
- 2 tsp. lemon extract
- 1/3 cup erythritol
- 4 oz. cream cheese, softened
- 1 cup butter, softened
- 2 tsp. xanthan gum
- 2 cups almond flour

Directions:
1. Preheat the oven to 325 F.
2. Grease a 9*5 loaf pan and set aside.
3. In a mixing bowl, mix together almond flour and xanthan gum, and set aside.
4. In a large bowl, beat cream cheese and butter until smooth. Add sweetener and lemon extract and beat until the mixture becomes fluffy.
5. Add eggs and eggs yolk one by one and beat until well combined.
6. Add almond flour mixture and beat until just combined. Do not over mix.
7. Pour batter into the prepared loaf pan and bake for 60 minutes.
8. Allow the cake to cool completely.
9. Slice and serve.

77. Simple Chocolate Cake

Prep Time: 10 minutes
Cooking Time: 14 minutes
Servings: 8
Ingredients:
- 3 eggs
- 1 1/2 tsp. vanilla
- 1/3 cup erythritol
- 1/3 cup almond milk
- 2 1/4 tsp. baking powder
- 1/4 cup unsweetened cocoa powder
- 1 1/2 cups almond flour
- Pinch of salt

Directions:
1. Preheat the oven to 350 F.
2. Grease an 8-inch cake pan and set aside.
3. Add all ingredients into the mixing bowl and mix until well combined.
4. Pour batter into the prepared cake pan and bake for 14 minutes.
5. Allow the cake to cool completely.
6. Slice and serve.

78. Perfect Pumpkin Crumb Cake

Prep Time: 10 minutes
Cooking Time: 40 minutes
Servings: 16
Ingredients:
- 2 eggs
- 1/2 tsp. vanilla
- 1/4 cup butter, melted
- 1/2 cup pumpkin puree
- 3/4 tsp. pumpkin pie spice
- 2 tsp. baking powder
- 1/4 cup whey protein powder
- 1/3 cup coconut flour
- 1/2 cup Swerve
- 1 cup almond flour
- Pinch of salt

For topping:
- 1 cup almond flour
- 1/2 cup butter, melted
- 1/2 tsp. pumpkin pie spice
- 1/2 cup Swerve
- 1/4 cup coconut flour
- Pinch of salt

Directions:
1. Preheat the oven to 325 F.
2. Grease a 9*9-inch cake pan and set aside.
3. Add all topping ingredients into a medium bowl and mix until well combined, and set aside.
4. Combine almond flour, pumpkin pie spice, baking soda, protein powder, coconut flour, sweetener, and salt in a large basin.
5. Stir in eggs, vanilla, butter, pumpkin puree until well combined.
6. Spoon the batter into the prepared cake pan and evenly distribute it. On top of the batter, evenly distribute the topping mixture.
7. Bake cake for 35-40 minutes.
8. Allow the cake to cool completely.
9. Slice and serve.

79. Carrot Cake with Frosting

Prep Time: 10 minutes
Cooking Time: 25 minutes
Servings: 12
Ingredients:
- 4 eggs
- 1/2 cup grated carrot
- 1/4 tsp. ground allspice
- 1 1/2 tsp. ground cinnamon
- 1 Tbsp. baking powder
- 2 Tbsp. coconut flour
- 1 1/2 cups almond flour
- 1 tsp. vanilla
- 2 Tbsp. almond milk
- 5 Tbsp. butter, softened
- 1/2 cup erythritol

For frosting:
- 4 oz. cream cheese, softened
- 1/4 cup erythritol
- 1 Tbsp. heavy cream
- 1 tsp. vanilla
- 2 Tbsp. butter, softened

Directions:
1. Preheat the oven to 350 F.
2. Grease a 9-inch cake pan and set aside.
3. In a large bowl, beat butter and sweetener until fluffy. Add eggs and beat well.
4. Add vanilla and almond milk and stir well.
5. Add spices, baking powder, coconut flour, and almond flour and beat until just combined.
6. Add grated carrot and fold well.
7. Pour the batter into the cake pan you have prepared and bake for 20-25 minutes.
8. Once done, remove from oven and set aside to cool completely.
9. For frosting: In a medium bowl, beat the cream cheese and butter until smooth. Add vanilla and sweetener and beat well.
10. Add heavy cream and stir well.
11. Once the cake is cool then spread the frosting on top.
12. Slice and serve.

80. Chocolate Flourless Cake

Prep Time: 10 minutes
Cooking Time: 45 minutes
Servings: 16
Ingredients:
- 6 eggs
- 1 Tbsp. vanilla
- 1/4 cup unsweetened cocoa powder
- 2 Tbsp. instant espresso powder
- 1 cup erythritol
- 10 oz. dark chocolate chips
- 5 oz. butter

Directions:
1. Preheat the oven to 350 F.
2. Grease an 8-inch springform pan and set aside.
3. Add chocolate chips and butter in a bowl and melt in a double boiler. Stir well.
4. Add espresso powder and sweetener and sit well.
5. Remove bowl from heat and let it cool for 10 minutes.
6. Add vanilla, cocoa powder, and eggs into the melted chocolate mixture and beat using a hand mixer until smooth.
7. Pour the batter into the cake pan you have prepared and bake for 45 minutes.
8. Allow the cake to cool completely.
9. Slice and serve.

81. Light & Fluffy Coffee Cake

Prep Time: 10 minutes
Cooking Time: 30 minutes
Servings: 12
Ingredients:
- 3 eggs
- 1/2 cup macadamia nuts, chopped
- 1/4 tsp. ground allspice
- 1 tsp. vanilla
- 1 tsp. baking powder
- 1 Tbsp. ground cinnamon
- 1/2 cup Swerve
- 1/4 cup almond flour
- 1/4 cup coconut flour
- 1/4 cup ground flax
- 1/2 cup sour cream
- 1/4 cup butter
- Pinch of salt

Directions:
1. Preheat the oven to 350 F.
2. Grease an 8*8-inch cake pan and set aside.
3. In a medium bowl, whisk eggs. Add cream and butter, and stir to combine.
4. In a separate bowl, mix together all dry ingredients.
5. Add the dry ingredient mixture into the egg mixture and blend until well combined.
6. Pour the batter into the cake pan you have prepared and bake for 30 minutes.
7. Allow the cake to cool completely.
8. Slice and serve.

82. Moist Coconut Pound Cake

Prep Time: 10 minutes
Cooking Time: 45 minutes
Servings: 8
Ingredients:
- 4 eggs
- 1 tsp. vanilla
- 1/2 cup coconut yogurt
- 1/2 cup Swerve
- 4 Tbsp. coconut oil
- 1 tsp. baking powder
- 1 1/4 cups almond flour
- Pinch of salt

Directions:
1. Preheat the oven to 350 F.
2. Grease an 8-inch loaf pan and set aside.
3. In a medium bowl, mix almond flour, baking powder, and salt together and set aside.
4. In a large mixing bowl, beat together the sweetener and coconut oil until light.
5. Add eggs, vanilla, and coconut yogurt and beat until well combined.
6. Add the almond flour mixture into the wet mixture and beat until just combined.
7. Pour the batter into the prepared loaf pan and bake for 40-5 minutes.
8. Allow the cake to cool completely.
9. Slice and serve.

83. Super Easy Chocolate Cake

Prep Time: 10 minutes
Cooking Time: 25 minutes
Servings: 8
Ingredients:
- 5 eggs
- 2/3 cup erythritol
- 2/3 cup butter, melted
- 9 oz. unsweetened dark chocolate
- 1 tsp. baking powder
- 1/2 cup almond flour
- 1 tsp. vanilla
- Pinch of salt

Directions:
1. Preheat the oven to 350 F.
2. Grease a cake pan and set aside.
3. In a mixing bowl, mix almond flour, baking powder, and salt together and set aside.
4. Melt butter and chocolate together. Stir well and let it cool.
5. Transfer the melted butter and chocolate mixture into the medium bowl.
6. Add eggs one by one and beat until smooth.
7. Add the almond flour mixture, sweetener, and vanilla and blend well.
8. Pour the batter into the cake pan you have prepared and bake for 20-25 minutes.
9. Allow the cake to cool completely.
10. Slice and serve.

84. Cream Cheese Pound Cake

Prep Time: 10 minutes
Cooking Time: 40 minutes
Servings: 12
Ingredients:
- 4 eggs
- 1 tsp. vanilla
- 4 Tbsp. butter
- 3.5 oz. cream cheese
- 1 tsp. baking powder
- 3/4 cup erythritol
- 1 1/4 cups almond flour
- Pinch of salt

Directions:
1. Preheat the oven to 350 F.
2. Grease an 8-inch loaf pan and set aside.
3. In a mixing bowl, mix almond flour, baking powder, and salt together and set aside.
4. In a large bowl, beat butter and sweetener until fluffy.
5. Add cream cheese and vanilla and mix well.
6. Add eggs one by one and beat well.
7. Add almond flour mixture and blend until well combined.
8. Pour the batter into the prepared loaf pan and bake for 30-40 minutes.
9. Allow the cake to cool completely.
10. Slice and serve.

85. Moist Vanilla Cake

Prep Time: 10 minutes
Cooking Time: 40 minutes
Servings: 8
Ingredients:
- 6 egg whites
- 1 tsp. baking powder
- 1/4 cup coconut flour
- 1 cup almond flour
- 1/2 cup Swerve
- 1/4 cup sour cream
- 1 tsp. vanilla
- 1/4 cup coconut oil, melted
- Pinch of salt

Directions:
1. Preheat the oven to 350 F.
2. Grease a loaf pan and set aside.
3. In a mixing bowl, whisk together vanilla and coconut oil. Add sour cream and whisk until combined.
4. Add sweetener and egg whites one by one and beat until combined.
5. Stir in the flours, baking powder, and salt, and blend until well combined.
6. Pour the batter into the prepared loaf pan and bake for 30-40 minutes.
7. Allow the cake to cool completely.
8. Slice and serve.

86. Perfect Blackberry Cake

Prep Time: 10 minutes
Cooking Time: 60 minutes
Servings: 16
Ingredients:
For cake:
- 4 eggs
- 1 tsp. vanilla
- 1/2 cup coconut milk
- 1/3 cup coconut milk, melted
- 1/2 cup Swerve
- 1 tsp. baking powder
- 1/4 cup coconut flour
- 1 1/4 cups almond flour

For topping:
- 2 Tbsp. coconut oil
- 2 Tbsp. Swerve
- 1 cup almonds
- 2 cups blackberries

Directions:
1. Preheat the oven to 350 F.
2. Grease an 8*8-inch cake pan and set aside.
3. For cake: In a medium bowl, mix together all the dry ingredients. Add the remaining cake ingredients and mix until well combined.
4. Pour the batter into the prepared cake pan. Sprinkle blackberries on top.
5. Bake the cake for 15 minutes.
6. Meanwhile, add almond, Swerve, and coconut oil into the food processor and process until a wet crumbly mixture is formed.
7. Sprinkle the crumb mixture on top of the cake and bake for 40-45 minutes more.
8. Allow the cake to cool completely.
9. Slice and serve.

87. Perfect Gingerbread Cake

Prep Time: 10 minutes
Cooking Time: 45 minutes
Servings: 12
Ingredients:
- 4 eggs
- 1/4 cup water
- 1/4 tsp. ground nutmeg
- 1/8 tsp. ground cloves
- 1 tsp. ground cinnamon
- 1 tsp. ground ginger
- 1 tsp. baking powder
- 2 Tbsp. psyllium husk powder
- 3/4 cup almond flour
- 1/4 cup coconut flour
- 1/2 cup Swerve
- 1/2 cup butter
- Pinch of salt

Directions:
1. Preheat the oven to 350 F.
2. Grease a 9-inch loaf pan and set aside.
3. In a large bowl, beat the butter and sweetener until fluffy.
4. Add eggs one by one and beat until well combined.
5. In a separate bowl, mix together the almond flour, cloves, nutmeg, cinnamon, ginger, baking powder, psyllium husk, coconut flour, and salt.
6. Add the almond flour mixture into the egg mixture and blend until well combined. Add water and stir until smooth.
7. Pour the batter into the prepared loaf pan and bake for 45 minutes.
8. Allow the cake to cool completely.
9. Slice and serve.

88. Chocolate Zucchini Cake

Prep Time: 10 minutes
Cooking Time: 30 minutes
Servings: 16
Ingredients:
- 3 eggs
- 3 Tbsp. coconut milk
- 3 Tbsp. coconut oil, melted
- 1/4 cup shredded zucchini
- 1/2 tsp. baking powder
- 1/4 tsp. baking soda
- 1/2 cup Swerve
- 1/4 cup unsweetened cocoa powder
- 1/4 cup coconut flour

Directions:
1. Preheat the oven to 350 F.
2. Grease an 8*8-inch cake pan and set aside.
3. Add all ingredients into the blender and blend until a thick batter forms.
4. Pour the batter into the prepared pan and bake for 25-30 minutes.
5. Allow the cake to cool completely.
6. Slice and serve.

89. Perfect Almond Crumb Cake

Prep Time: 10 minutes
Cooking Time: 40 minutes
Servings: 16
Ingredients:
For cake:
- 4 eggs
- 1 tsp. baking powder
- 1 cup almond flour
- 1/2 cup coconut flour
- 4 oz. half and half
- 2 tsp. vanilla
- 1/3 cup Swerve
- 2 oz. cream cheese, softened
- 2 Tbsp. butter

For topping:
- 1 cup sliced almonds, toasted
- 1 cup almond flour
- 1/3 cup Swerve
- 6 Tbsp. butter, melted

Directions:
1. Preheat the oven to 350 F.
2. Grease an 8*8-inch cake pan and set aside.
3. Add all cake ingredients into the large mixing bowl and beat until well combined.
4. Pour the batter into the prepared cake pan. Mix together all the topping ingredients and sprinkle on top of the cake batter.
5. Bake it for 40 minutes.
6. Allow the cake to cool completely.
7. Slice and serve.

90. Lemon Pound Cake

Prep Time: 10 minutes
Cooking Time: 40 minutes
Servings: 8
Ingredients:
- 4 eggs
- 1 Tbsp. lemon zest
- 2 tsp. baking powder
- 2 cups almond flour
- 1/4 cup sour cream
- 1 tsp. lemon extract
- 3/4 cup Swerve
- 4 Tbsp. butter, softened
- 4 oz. cream cheese
- 1 lemon juice

Directions:
1. Preheat the oven to 350 F.
2. Grease a cake pan and set aside.
3. In a mixing bowl, beat together the butter, sweetener, and cream cheese until fluffy.
4. Add lemon juice and lemon extract, and stir well.
5. Add sour cream and eggs, and mix well.
6. Add all the dry ingredients and beat until well combined.
7. Pour the batter into the cake pan you have prepared and bake for 40 minutes.
8. Allow the cake to cool completely.
9. Slice and serve.

91. Blueberry Cake

Prep Time: 10 minutes
Cooking Time: 40 minutes
Servings: 10
Ingredients:

For cake:
- 2 eggs
- 1 1/2 tsp. baking powder
- 1/2 cup coconut flour
- 1 tsp. vanilla
- 1/2 cup butter, softened

For filling:
- 1 cup blueberries
- 1/3 cup xylitol
- 1 tsp. vanilla
- 3 eggs
- 1 cup sour cream

Directions:
1. Preheat the oven to 350 F.
2. Grease an 8-inch springform pan and set aside.
3. In a mixing bowl, beat butter and sweetener until light. Add vanilla and egg one by one and beat until well combined.
4. Mix together the coconut flour and baking powder, then add into the egg mixture and blend until well combined.
5. Pour the batter into the prepared pan and set aside.
6. For the filling: In a large bowl, whip sour cream, sweetener, vanilla, and eggs until creamy. Pour over the cake batter.
7. Sprinkle blueberries evenly on top of cake batter.
8. Bake the cake for 35-40 minutes.
9. Allow the cake to cool completely.
10. Slice and serve.

92. Brownie Mug Cake

Prep Time: 10 minutes
Cooking Time: 2 minutes
Servings: 1
Ingredients:
- 1 egg
- 1 Tbsp. unsweetened chocolate chips
- 1/2 tsp. baking powder
- 1 Tbsp. unsweetened cocoa powder
- 1 Tbsp. Swerve
- 1/4 cup almond flour
- 1 Tbsp. butter, melted

Directions:
1. Add all ingredients into the microwave-safe mug and stir until well combined.
2. Place in the microwave and microwave for 2 minutes.
3. Serve and enjoy.

93. Peanut Butter Mug Cake

Prep Time: 10 minutes
Cooking Time: 1 minute
Servings: 6
Ingredients:
- 3 Tbsp. unsweetened chocolate chips
- 1/4 cup water
- 1/2 tsp. vanilla
- 2 eggs
- 2 tsp. baking powder
- 1/3 cup Swerve
- 2/3 cup almond flour
- 1/4 cup butter
- 1/3 cup peanut butter

Directions:
1. Melt butter and peanut butter in a microwave-safe bowl. Stir until smooth.
2. In a medium bowl, mix together almond flour, baking powder, and sweetener. Stir in melted butter mixture, eggs, and vanilla.
3. Add water and stir until well combined. Add chocolate chips and stir well.
4. Divide the mixture into 6 ramekins and microwave for 1 minute.
5. Serve warm and enjoy.

94. Vanilla Mug Cake

Prep Time: 10 minutes
Cooking Time: 1 minute
Servings: 1
Ingredients:
- 1 egg
- 1/4 tsp. baking powder
- 1/4 tsp. vanilla
- 1 Tbsp. Swerve
- 1 Tbsp. coconut flour
- 1 oz. cream cheese, softened

Directions:
1. In a small bowl, whisk egg, cream cheese, and vanilla for 2 minutes.
2. Add remaining ingredients and stir until well combined.
3. Pour this mixture into a microwave-safe mug and microwave for 1 minute.
4. Serve warm and enjoy.

95. Delicious Berry Cake

Prep Time: 10 minutes
Cooking Time: 1 minute
Servings: 1
Ingredients:
- 1 egg
- 5 frozen raspberries
- 1/4 tsp. baking powder
- 1 tsp. vanilla
- 1 Tbsp. Swerve
- 2 Tbsp. coconut flour
- 2 Tbsp. cream cheese
- 1 Tbsp. butter, melted

Directions:
1. Add all ingredients except raspberries into a microwave-safe mug and whisk until smooth.
2. Add raspberries and stir well.
3. Microwave on high for 80 seconds.
4. Serve and enjoy.

96. Quick Microwave Cheesecake

Prep Time: 10 minutes
Cooking Time: 2 minutes
Servings: 1
Ingredients:
- 1 egg
- 1/2 tsp. stevia
- 1/4 tsp. vanilla
- 2 oz. cream cheese, cubed

Directions:
1. Add cream cheese into the ramekin and microwave for 15 seconds to soften.
2. Add sweetener and vanilla, and stir to combine.
3. Add egg and stir until smooth.
4. Microwave for 90 seconds.
5. Let it cool completely then serve.

97. Easy Lemon Cheesecake

Prep Time: 10 minutes
Cooking Time: 55 minutes
Servings: 8
Ingredients:
- 4 eggs
- 2 Tbsp. erythritol
- 1/4 tsp. lemon extract
- 1 fresh lemon juice
- 18 oz. ricotta cheese
- 1 fresh lemon zest

Directions:
1. Preheat the oven to 350 F.
2. Grease a cake pan and set aside.
3. In a large bowl, beat ricotta cheese until smooth.
4. Add egg one by one and whisk well. Add lemon juice, lemon extract, lemon zest, and sweetener and mix well.
5. Pour the batter in the prepared cake pan and bake for 50-55 minutes.
6. Let it cool completely, then place in the refrigerator for 2 hours.
7. Slice and serve.

98. Delicious & Healthy Pumpkin Cheesecake

Prep Time: 10 minutes
Cooking Time: 70 minutes
Servings: 8
Ingredients:
For Crust:
- 1/2 cup almond flour
- 1 Tbsp. flaxseed meal
- 1 Tbsp. erythritol
- 1/4 cup butter, melted

For Filling:
- 3 eggs
- 15.5 oz. cream cheese
- 1/4 tsp. nutmeg
- 2/3 cup erythritol
- 1/2 tsp. ground cinnamon
- 1/2 tsp. vanilla
- 2/3 cup pumpkin puree
- Pinch of salt

Directions:
1. Preheat the oven to 300 F.
2. Grease a 9-inch springform pan. Set aside.
3. For Crust: In a bowl, mix together almond flour, sweetener, flaxseed meal, and salt. Add melted butter and mix well to combine.
4. Transfer the crust mixture into the prepared pan and press firmly, then bake for 10-15 minutes.
5. Remove from the oven and let it cool for 10 minutes.
6. For filling: In a large bowl, beat cream cheese until smooth.
7. Add eggs, vanilla, sweetener, pumpkin puree, nutmeg, cinnamon, and salt and stir until well combined.
8. Pour the batter into the prepared crust and spread evenly and bake for 50-55 minutes.
9. Remove the cheesecake from the oven and set aside to cool completely.
10. Let it cool completely before placing it in the refrigerator for 4 hours.
11. Slice and serve.

99. Almond Coconut Cheesecake

Prep Time: 10 minutes
Cooking Time: 80 minutes
Servings: 8
Ingredients:
- 3 eggs
- 1 tsp. vanilla
- 1 Tbsp. stevia
- 15.5 oz. sour cream
- 8 oz. cream cheese, softened
- 1/2 cup butter, melted
- 1/4 cup shredded coconut
- 1/2 cup coconut flour
- 1/2 cup almond flour

Directions:
1. Preheat the oven 300 F.
2. Grease a 9-inch springform pan. Set aside.
3. For the crust: In a mixing bowl, mix together coconut flour, almond flour, shredded coconut, and butter until well combined.
4. Transfer the crust mixture into the prepared pan, spread evenly and press firmly.
5. Place the pan into the freezer to set crust.
6. For the filling: In a large bowl, beat sour cream and cream cheese together.
7. Add egg, vanilla, and sweetener and beat until well combined.
8. Pour filling evenly over crust and bake for 1 hour 20 minutes.
9. Remove the cake pan from oven and set aside to cool completely.
10. Let it cool completely before placing it in the refrigerator for 6 hours.
11. Slice and serve.

100. Almond Cake

Prep Time: 10 minutes
Cooking Time: 40 minutes
Servings: 16
Ingredients:
- 4 eggs
- 2 Tbsp. butter
- 1 1/2 cups almond flour
- 4 oz. half and half
- 1 tsp. baking powder
- 1 1/2 tsp. vanilla
- 1/3 cup erythritol
- 2 oz. cream cheese, softened
- Pinch of salt

For the topping:
- 3/4 cup almonds, toasted and sliced
- 1 cup almond flour
- 1/3 cup erythritol
- 6 Tbsp. butter, melted

Directions:
1. Preheat the oven to 350 F.
2. Grease an 8-inch cake pan and set aside.
3. Add all ingredients except the topping ingredients into the large bowl, and whisk to combine.
4. Pour the batter into the prepared cake pan and spread evenly.
5. Mix together all topping ingredients and sprinkle on top of batter.
6. Bake for 40 minutes.
7. Remove from oven and allow to cool completely.
8. Chill in the refrigerator, then slice and serve.

101. Moist Vanilla Cake

Prep Time: 10 minutes
Cooking Time: 35 minutes
Servings: 9
Ingredients:
- 5 eggs
- 1 cup Swerve
- 4 oz. cream cheese, softened
- 1 tsp. vanilla
- 1 tsp. baking powder
- 6.5 oz. almond flour
- 1/2 cup butter, softened

Directions:
1. Preheat the oven to 350 F.
2. Grease a 9-inch cake pan and set aside.
3. Add all ingredients into the mixing bowl and whisk until fluffy.
4. Pour batter into the prepared pan and bake for 35-40 minutes.
5. Let it cool completely then slice and serve.

102. Basic Cheese Cake

Prep Time: 15 minutes
Cooking Time: 15 minutes
Servings: 10
Ingredients:
- 16 oz. cream cheese
- 1 cup Swerve
- 1 tsp. vanilla
- 3/4 cup heavy cream
- 1/2 cup sour cream

For crust:
- 2 cups almond flour
- 1 tsp. vanilla
- 3 Tbsp. swerve
- 1/3 cup butter, melted

Directions:
1. Preheat the oven to 350 F.
2. For the crust: In a bowl, mix together almond flour, vanilla, Swerve, and butter until combined.
3. Add the crust mixture into the 9-inch cake pan and spread evenly. Bake for 10-15 minutes.
4. For the filling: In a mixing bowl, beat together cream cheese, vanilla, and sweetener until creamy.
5. Add heavy cream and sour cream and beat for 2 minutes.
6. Pour filling mixture on top of crust and spread evenly. Place cheesecake in the freezer for 1 hour.
7. Slice and serve.

103. Quick & Easy Cheesecake

Prep Time: 10 minutes
Cooking Time: 10 minutes
Servings: 2
Ingredients:
- 2 eggs
- 1/2 tsp. fresh lemon juice
- 1 tsp. vanilla
- 3/4 cup erythritol
- 16 oz. cream cheese, softened
- 2 Tbsp. sour cream

Directions:
1. Preheat the air fryer to 350 F.
2. Add eggs, lemon juice, vanilla, and sweetener in a large bowl and beat until smooth.
3. Add cream cheese and sour cream and beat until fluffy.
4. Pour the batter into the 2 4-inch springform pan and place in air fryer basket and cook for 10 minutes at 350 F.
5. Let it cool completely before placing it in the refrigerator for 8 hours.
6. Serve and enjoy.

104. Italian Cheesecake

Prep time: 25 minutes
Cooking Time: 2 hours 30 minutes
Ready In: 7 hours

Ingredients

- 230 grams of cream cheese
- 456 grams of ricotta cheese
- 2 cups refined sugar
- 8 small eggs
- 3 tsp. lemon juice
- ¼ Tbsp. vanilla extract
- 9 tsp. cornstarch
- 5 Tbsp. all-purpose flour
- ¾ cup melted butter
- A small amount of sour cream

Directions

1. Prepare the oven by preheating it to 360 degrees Fahrenheit. While waiting, grease the springform pan to be used.
2. In a large bowl, combine the two kinds of cheese. Add the lemon juice, eggs, flour, sugar, cornstarch, and the melted butter. Mix well. Now add in the sour cream and mix well. Transfer the mixture into the baking pan.
3. Place the pan in the oven and bake for an hour. Let it cool but do not take it out from the oven.
4. Do this for another hour. When done, place it in the refrigerator to cool.

105. Italian Creamy Cake

Prep Time: 10 minutes
Cooking Time: 45 minutes
Servings: 3
Ingredients
- ¾ cup of softened butter
- ¾ cup of shortening
- 2 ½ cup of refined sugar
- 7 egg yolks
- 3 cups of flour
- ¾ Tbsp. of baking soda
- ¾ cup of buttermilk
- ½ Tbsp. of vanilla extract
- 1 ½ cups of flaked coconut
- 1 ½ cups of pecans, chopped
- 7 egg whites
- 227 grams of cream cheese
- ½ cup of butter, softened
- 5 cups of confectioners' sugar

Directions
1. Prepare the oven by preheating it to 360 degrees Fahrenheit. While waiting, grease some cake pans and flour each.
2. Whisk egg whites to form peaks.
3. Cream ¾ cup of butter together with the shortening using a medium-sized bowl. Add in the refined sugar followed by the yolks, baking soda, flour, and buttermilk. Mix well. Then add a tsp. of flaked coconut and vanilla extract including a cup of grounded pecans. Fold. Scoop some mixture and place it in the pans prepared.
4. Place the pan in the oven for about 30 to 45 minutes. Let it cool for 15 minutes before removing from the oven.
5. Mix the powdered sugar with the cream cheese, a tsp. of vanilla extract, and butter in another bowl. Mix well. Use this mixture to frost the cake. You can also use the remaining pecans for garnishing the cake.

106. Sicilian Layer Cake

Prep time: 40 minutes
Cooking Time: 30 minutes
Servings: 3
Ingredients:
- 1 ¼ cups of buttermilk
- ¼ Tbsp. of baking soda
- 1 ½ cups of sugar (white)
- ¾ cup of butter
- ¾ cup of vegetable oil
- ¼ cup of shortening
- 5 yolks
- ¼ Tbsp. of vanilla extract
- 5 egg whites
- 2 ½ cups of flour
- 100 grams of flaked coconut
- ¾ cup of pecans (chopped)
- 0.5 lb. of cream cheese
- ¾ cup of margarine
- 3 cups of confectioners' sugar
- ¼ Tbsp. of vanilla extract
- ¾ cup pecans (chopped)

Directions
1. Heat the oven to 350 degrees Fahrenheit while applying grease to the pans. Mix the buttermilk and soda. Set aside.
2. Take out a bowl and mix the shortening, oil, butter, and sugar. Add the yolks one by one, whisking after every addition. Pour in the flour, buttermilk mixture and vanilla to the cream mixture.
3. Whisk egg whites and pour them to the batter. Lightly add coconuts and pecans.
4. Transfer batter to the pans and bake for 20 to 25 minutes. Set aside to cool.
5. For the frosting, mix the remaining ingredients and top onto the cakes. Freeze and serve after.

107. Ricotta Cinnamon Cheesecake

Prep Time: 10 minutes
Cooking Time: 60 minutes
Servings: 3
Ingredients:
- 1 kilogram of ricotta cheese
- ½ cup of sugar (white)
- ½ cup of flour
- 7 eggs
- ½ tsp. Teaspoon of cinnamon
- 1 Tbsp. of orange zest
- 1 Tbsp. of vanilla extract
- 5 dashes of salt

Directions
1. Heat the oven to 320 degrees Fahrenheit while applying flour and butter to the pan.
2. Mix all the ingredients in a large bowl. For the eggs, just add one by one.
3. Bake for an hour or until it gets a golden brown color. Once done, let it cool. Serve when fully cooled.

108. Blueberry Cheese Squares

Prep time: 35 minutes
Cooking Time: 55 minutes
Servings: 3

Ingredients
- 1 ½ cup of flour
- 1 cup of sugar (white)
- 1 Tbsp. of baking powder
- ¼ cup of milk
- 1/3 cup of shortening
- 1 Tbsp. of flax seed
- ¼ Tbsp. of lemon extract
- 1 cup of blueberries
- 2 Tbsp. of flax seed
- 1 cup of nut cheese
- ¼ cup of sugar (white)
- ½ Tbsp. of vanilla extract

Directions
1. Heat up the oven to 370 degrees Fahrenheit while greasing the baking sheet.
2. In a large container, mix the first 7 ingredients using a mixer for 2 minutes. Pour evenly on the baking sheet and scatter the blueberries on top.
3. In a different container, mix the remaining ingredients and pour this on top of the blueberries.
4. Bake this for 50 to 55 minutes. Let it cool, then serve.

109. Chocolate Italian Cream Cake

Prep Time: 10 minutes
Cooking Time: 50 minutes
Servings: 3
Ingredients
- ¾ cup of olive oil
- ¾ cup of shortening
- 3 cups of sugar (white)
- 5 egg whites and egg yolks
- 3 cups of all-purpose flour
- 2 tsp. of baking soda
- ½ cup of cocoa powder (unsweetened)
- ½ cup of buttermilk
- 1 Tbsp. of vanilla extract
- ¾ cup of coconut (shredded)
- 1 ½ cups of pecans (chopped)
- 3/4 cup of nut cheese
- 1 cup of butter
- 1/3 cup of cocoa powder (unsweetened)
- 5 cups of confectioners' sugar
- 1 ½ cups of pecans (chopped)
- 2 tsp. of vanilla extract

Directions:
1. Heat up the oven to 360 degrees Fahrenheit while applying oil and flour to the round pans.
2. Mix the olive oil, sugar, and shortening. Then add the yolks one by one after each beating. Pour in the vanilla extract.
3. Sift together the cocoa, soda, and flour. Then add this to the cream mixture together with the buttermilk. Also, add the dry ingredients.
4. Whisk the egg whites until peaks are obtained. Fold into the batter. Place the batter into the cake pans.
5. Bake the cakes over a 320 degrees Fahrenheit heat for 30 to 35 minutes. Once done, set aside to let it cool.
6. For the frostings, mix the cheese and butter together. Add sugar and cocoa then beat to mix well. Lastly, add some pecans and 2 tsps. vanilla extract. Pour it over the cake then serve.

110. Italian Anniversary Cake

Prep time: 1 hour
Cooking Time: 40 minutes
Servings: 1
Ingredients:
- ¾ cup of buttermilk
- ½ Tbsp. of baking soda
- ¼ Tbsp. of salt
- ¼ cup of shortening
- ¼ cup of margarine
- 1 ¾ of white sugar
- 6 yolks
- ½ tsp. of almond extract
- 2 tsp. of vanilla extract
- 2 ½ of cup flour
- 6 egg whites
- ¼ cup of crushed pineapple (drained)
- ¼ cup of crumbled coconut
- 2 cups of pecans (chopped)
- 1 cup of olive oil
- 223 grams of softened cream cheese
- 5 cups of confectioners' sugar
- 1 Tbsp. of vanilla extract

Directions
1. Heat the oven to 370 degrees Fahrenheit while combining the salt, baking soda, and the buttermilk. Sprinkle flour onto 3 pans.
2. Get a large bowl and mix the following; sugar, margarine, shortening, egg yolks, flour, buttermilk mixture, vanilla, and almond extract. In a different bowl, whip the egg whites. Pour into the previous bowl together with the pecans, coconut, and pineapple.
3. Pour evenly into the pans and bake for 40 minutes. Once done, let it cool while making a frosting.
4. For the frosting, blend the confectioner's sugar, oil, and cheese. Add a Tbsp. of vanilla and pour the pecans. Spread this over the cake and then serve.

CHAPTER 5: FAQs

What Ingredient Substitutions can you make?

There are endless options for ingredient substitutions. Most notable are the lower calorie, or non-fat versions. One substitution <u>not recommended</u> is to use whipped cream cheese for the solid block.
Here are a few possible substitutions:
Filling:
- Light, reduced or low fat cream cheese
- Egg substitutes such as Ener-G Egg Replacer
- Skim, low or non-fat sweetened condensed milk
- Smart balance spread in place of butter
- 60-70% dark or bittersweet chocolate
- Truvia for white sugar – one for one or equal amount
- Almond extract in place of vanilla extract
- Ricotta cheese (Italian style) for cream cheese

Crust:
- Store bought premade crust
- Gluten-Free Graham Crackers for traditional Graham Crackers
- Chocolate Graham Crackers
- Ginger Snaps
- Oreo Thin Crips
- Vanilla Wafers
- Chocolate cookies
- Pecan sandies cookies
- Vanilla wafers

How to do a Perfect Crust Presentation?

Traditionally, cheesecake will have crust along the sides. Although I have not noted in most of these recipes to press the crust up the sides of the pan, you can certainly do this if you prefer. If you like the idea of a crusted side then it is recommended you press the crust anywhere from 1 to 1 ½ inches up the greased side of the pan. When deciding on a crusted side, consider the topping you may wish to use and if you plan on covering the sides with the topping or not.

How to do Proper Processing / Mixing?

If you intend to serve the cheesecake in a different cake or pie dish, cut out and line the bottom of the baking pan with parchment paper, and then cut separate pieces to line the sides.

Crust: The quickest and simplest way to make crumbs is to seal your favorite crust in a zip lock bag and gently pound down until fine and medium fine crumbs form. A food processor is another option for making crumbs. Tamp the crust mixture to a mild firmness with a wide bottom glass. Some recipes may suggest baking the crust alone for about 10 minutes. This is known as blind baking. I'm really ambivalent about this practice, and I don't usually do it because I believe it can cause extra crust hardening.

Filling: Bring all refrigerated ingredients, including eggs, butter, cream cheese, and cream, to room temperature before mixing. This allows for more thorough mixing and the avoidance of lumps. It is best to use an electric mixer with a paddle attachment. Most ingredients should be blended at slow to medium speeds, with the exception of sugar or other powdered ingredients, which should be blended at high speeds. Add the next ingredient only after the previous one has been thoroughly blended into the mixture. This includes incorporating one egg at a time.

Add the eggs last and only blend enough to incorporate the eggs.

The filling mixture should not be over-beaten. It will increase the risk of cracking while baking by adding more air.

After pouring the cream cheese filling batter into your crusted pan, tap the bottom or gently shake the pan to level the filling.

How to Master Times and Temperatures?

Baking times and temperatures vary across the recipes. Most call for anywhere from 45 minutes to 1 hour of baking. I recommend not depending absolutely on the temperature or time recommended in the recipes due to variations in ovens.

How to Know Signs of Doneness?

Keep an eye on the cheesecake at 34% of the recommended time and look for signs of doneness. These indicators include puffy, lightly browned edges, and a center that is firm but still wobbles or jiggles when the pan is gently moved. Overbaking the cheesecake is common, so pay close attention near the end of the baking time.

Other methods for determining doneness include using an instant-read probe thermometer or inserting a small knife into the center. If the knife comes out clean, the cake is finished. The ideal temperature for the probe thermometer, which is inserted into the center, is around 160 to 165 degrees F. (70 to 72 degrees C).

Once you've determined that the cheesecake is done, turn off the oven and prop the door open for approximately 1 hour. This allows residual heat to continue baking and the center to continue to cook mildly. After an hour in the oven, remove the cheesecake and set it out at room temperature for another 30 minutes before placing it in the refrigerator. The center will firm up after the residual cooking and complete chilling in the refrigerator.

After the pan has finished cooling, carefully run a small knife or metal spatula around the edge or rim of the pan to loosen any bits that may have stuck to the pan. Remove the side of the spring form pan only after it has completely chilled.

How Can You Prevent Cracking?

The most common issue that cheesecake bakers face is the heartbreak of cracked cheesecake. While the cracking has no effect on the taste of the cheesecake, it does detract from its overall appearance.

Cheesecakes typically crack for one of two reasons: too much beating before baking (which causes the entrapment of air in the mixture); the air is released during the bake cycle, and the cheesecake collapses and cracks, similar to a souffle; or Inadequate post-bake cooling time before removing from the oven. The cheesecake, like a souffle, is a delicate creation that can easily crack if removed from the oven while the batter/cake is still warm.

Here are a few solutions I've tried that, alone or in combination, have reduced the number of cracked cheesecakes I've made.

Do not over-mix the batter. Allow the mixture to stand in the refrigerator for a half-hour, then remove it from the refrigerator and allow it to stand for another half-hour before placing it in the preheated oven.

After baking, leave the cheesecake in the oven with the door closed and the heat turned off for an hour. At the end of the baking time, simply turn off the heat without opening the door.

If that isn't enough, bake the cheesecake in a water bath.

Run a knife around the inner edge of the springform pan to loosen the cheesecake from the pan at the end of the cool-down period, then allow the cheesecake to cool completely at room temperature. Refrigerate the springform sides for at least six hours before removing them.

If all else fails and your cheesecake cracks, cover it with a can of cherries or blueberries to hide the cracks. (Hey, even the best of us laugh now and then!)

Over-blending or mixing causes air bubbles in the batter; over-baking causes the eggs to over-coagulate, causing the proteins to shrink when cooled; and too drastic a temperature change - usually from cooling down too quickly.

Following the blending and doneness assessment recommendations outlined above will help to reduce cracking from the first two causes. A drastic temperature change is more difficult to control, so baking the cheesecake in a water bath is the best crack prevention technique. Water protects the cheesecake from high heat, preventing it from drying out, and it regulates the rate at which heat moves into the cheesecake. Water absorbs a lot of energy while remaining at the same temperature, slowing the rate of heating and cooling. Water also helps to keep the oven moist and the heating process gentle.

A water bath, in my opinion, is only necessary if you do not intend to use a thick topping to cover any cracks. It makes no difference in the taste or texture of the cheesecake. You can also reduce the cracking effect by adding 1 Tbsp. of cornstarch or flour to the filling mixture at the same time as the sugar. The molecules of cornstarch or flour bind between the egg proteins, preventing them from over-coagulating.

How to Make a Water Bath:
- Bring 2 quarts of water to a boil in a teakettle that is easy to pour. If using a springform pan, wrap the bottom and sides with heavy aluminum foil to minimize the mess in case of leaking. Whether you're using a water bath or not, find a pan that's similar in shape but larger and deeper than your baking, pie, or springform pan. (the larger pan should be at least 2-3 inches deep). Spread a small towel in the bottom of this larger pan to act as an insulator and prevent hot water splashing. Place your cheesecake pan into the larger pan off to one side to allow space to pour in the hot water.
- Place the two pans together on the middle rack of a preheated oven.
- Pour the hot water from the kettle slowly into one side of the larger pan, about 2/3 of the way up the side of the cheesecake pan. Reposition the cheesecake in the center of the water bath.
- Close the oven door and bake as directed.

How to Master Topping Presentation?

One basic presentation rule to keep in mind - if you choose a recipe that has a flavored cheesecake center or filling, your topping should represent that flavor, fruit etc. For example, the chocolate raspberry cheesecake should be topped with both raspberry sauce or preserves and maybe chocolate chips and / or chocolate sauce drizzled on top. This provides the consumer with a better overall picture of your cheesecake theme.

The topping can be as simple or as artistic as you feel or are comfortable with. There are no hard rules for decorating and sometimes just simple pouring over, drizzling, or tossing on the topping provides the most artistic of presentations.

One last note: If you need to cover seams along the sides prior to topping, you can smooth the sides with a hot, wet knife.

How to Prepare the Cheesecake for Serving?

If you used a springform pan, unclip the clasp and remove the sides after the cake has completely chilled and before topping and/or serving. Follow these steps before topping the cheesecake if you want to serve it on a special serving plate.

Transfer the cake from a Springform Pan to a Serving Plate:

1. If you haven't already, run a small knife around the sides of the cheesecake to ensure it isn't sticking to the sides.

2. Remove the sides of the springform pan and place a piece of wax paper on top of the cheesecake. Place the bottom of another springform pan or other flat round or flat bottom pan or plate over the top of the cheesecake and wax paper.

3. Invert the cheesecake onto a flat-bottomed pan or plate lined with wax paper.

4. Gently separate the crust from the pan by running a warm knife under the bottom pan piece.

5. Place your serving plate on the cheesecake's now-exposed crusted bottom.

6. Pick up and turn the cheesecake over, then remove the top pan and slowly peel off the wax paper.

Transfer the cake from the baking pan to a serving plate:

1. After the cheesecake pan has been completely chilled, place it in a hot tap water bath in the sink for a minute to melt the butter at the bottom of the pan.

2. Using a knife, trace around the parchment paper on the sides of the cheesecake and carefully peel away the side paper.

3. Place a piece of wax paper on top of the cheesecake, then place the bottom of a springform pan or other flat round or flat bottom pan or plate over the cheesecake and wax paper.

4. Invert the cheesecake onto the wax paper-lined pan or plate with a flat bottom.

5. Remove the parchment paper from the cheesecake's bottom.

6. Place your serving plate on the crusted bottom that is now exposed.

7. Pick up and turn the cheesecake over, then remove the top pan and slowly peel off the wax paper.

Place the cheesecake on a serving plate and top with your preferred topping, fruit, or garnish.

The typical 9-10 inch springform or baking pie pan can be cut into 12 pieces. A good pattern to follow to get at least 12 pieces is to follow the hours on a clock, cutting across like a pizza or individually.

How to apply the Recipe Conversion Factors?

There are various specific size pans to put in mind. Typically, it's the nine (9) inch springform pan, unless otherwise specified.

If you don't mind a slightly thinner cake, you can just use the same recipe and cut down on the cooking time a bit. If you want the same thickness of the cake, then the volume of batter you'll need will have to be corrected for the different areas of the pans:

12-inch pan - approximately 113 square inches

11-inch pan - approximately 95 square inches

10-inch pan - approximately 78 square inches

9-inch pan - approximately 63 square inches

8-inch pan - approximately 50 square inches

7-inch pan - approximately 38 square inches

To a precision satisfactory for most recipes, a 10-inch pan requires one and a half times as much batter as an 8-inch pan, and one and a quarter-time as much as a 9-inch pan.

So, you can adjust your recipes accordingly. The only problem with adjusting cheesecake recipes is that you sometimes wind up needing a quarter of an egg. First, remember that it's not that critical to get the conversion precisely right, and secondly, decide whether you want to round the eggs up to the nearest whole egg or down to the nearest whole egg based on the effects of eggs on the batter.

In general, egg whites both lighten a cheesecake and toughen the texture; egg yolks make the cake firmer but don't lighten. The yolks also lend a "rich" taste to the cake. So, if you need part of an egg, you can separate it and use whichever half you prefer, or you can use one less egg for a softer, heavier cake or one more egg for a firmer, lighter cake.

CONCLUSION

Thank you for reading this book. Cheesecakes are one of the simplest and most delicious cakes to make. But don't be worried if your cheesecake does not appear "perfect."

With the help of this book, you can now make a fantastic cheesecake for birthdays, anniversaries, christenings, or any other occasion. Why not impress your friends the next time they have a birthday or other celebration by bringing one of your cheesecake creations to share? Cheesecakes aren't just for dessert; they can be eaten at any time, anywhere.

Cheesecakes come in a wide range of flavors, including soft and creamy fillings, delectable toppings, and complementary garnishes. Fresh fruit or chopped nuts add an elegant touch to a simple dish that everyone will enjoy.

The next step is for you to start making all of the delectable cheesecakes using the recipes from this book. After that, all you have to do is take what you've learned from this book and continue to make any kind of cheesecake recipe you can find.

This cookbook is written to satisfy all of your cheesecake desires and demands, so you won't have to look elsewhere for recipes for the various flavors you crave. Make these desserts for your family and friends at a gathering or just to brighten their day. The best part about these cheesecake recipes is that they don't use any difficult-to-find ingredients. It's all very simple.

You can try any of these recipes whenever you want, or you can learn any of them by following the instructions in this cheesecake recipes cookbook, as we have done our best to provide you with all of the assistance you require. We hope we were able to assist you in every way you desired. We hope you enjoy trying these recipes and making your family happy.

Cheesecakes are delicious at any time of year and are an excellent choice for special occasions and holidays. The best part is that not all cheesecakes have to be dessert. There are recipes, such as those in this book, that make cheesecake the star of the show. Combine vegetables and meats to create a crowd-pleasing dish that even kids will enjoy.

Without a doubt, cheesecake is one of the best desserts ever. It's smooth and heavy, but it's not difficult to swallow. Nonetheless, it may be difficult to create one. To make the perfect cheesecake, you must master, or at least be familiar with, the steps. Remember that one wrong move can ruin your delicious cheesecake. Good luck.

ALPHABETICAL INDEX

B
Best Ever Cheesecake, 71
Black Forest Cheesecake, 74
Blueberry Cheese Squares, 145
Blueberry Cheesecake, 108
Brown Sugar Amaretto Cheesecake, 77
Butterfinger Cheesecake, 80

C
Candy Cane Cheesecake, 83
Caramel Cheesecake Bars, 95
Chocolate Cheesecake, 46
Chocolate Cupcakes With Pumpkin Cheesecake Filling, 59
Chocolate Flourless Cake, 119
Classic Pound Cake, 112
Coconut Cardamom Cheesecake, 26
Cranberry Grape Cheesecake, 28

D
Delicious & Healthy Pumpkin Cheesecake, 135
Delicious Berry Cake, 133
Delicious Chocó Cheesecake, 102
Double Crusted Pumpkin Chocolate Cheesecake, 32

E
Easy Sour Cream Cheesecake, 63

F
Fig Hazelnut Cheesecake With Honey Bourbon Drizzle, 65

I
Italian Anniversary Cake, 147

L
Lemon Berry Swirl Cheesecake, 35
Lemon Cheesecake, 99
Lemon Pound Cake, 115

M
Mango and Coconut Cheesecake, 13
Mixed Berry Cheesecake, 14

N
Nutella Oreo Cheesecake, 51

P
Perfect Almond Crumb Cake, 128
Perfect Blackberry Cake, 125
Perfect Pumpkin Crumb Cake, 117
Pineapple Cheesecake, 17
Pistachio Cheesecake, 56
Pumpkin Cheesecake Bars, 93

Q
Quick & Easy Cheesecake, 140

R
Red Velvet cheesecake, 22
Ricotta Lemon Cheesecake, 106

S
Strawberry Cheesecake (with a few raspberries), 19
Super Easy Chocolate Cake, 122

T
Tiramisu with Vanilla Cream and Coffee Ladyfingers, 38
Triple Chocolate Cheesecake, 87

V
Vanilla Lemon Cheesecake, 4

Manufactured by Amazon.ca
Bolton, ON